# Stop!!!

This program cannot be used effectively without online registration.

*Without online registration, you won't have access to practice tests, answer sheets, detailed explanations, automated scoring, personalized study plans.*

Before moving forward, please complete your registration using the information given below.

## Complete Your Registration Now

Scan the QR Code or Visit

**lumoslearning.com/a/tedbooks**

Use Access Code: TMG6ELA-19428-P

# How to Use the Lumos Program?

Congratulations on choosing the Lumos Test Mastery Program! This isn't just a book. It's a comprehensive program designed to help your child succeed on the state test.

**Here is how to use the program:**

1. Login to your child's account at *lumoslearning.com* using the details sent to your registered email.

2. Have your child take the assigned online Practice Test 1.

3. After finishing the test, click on the *View Study Plan* button on the home page.

4. For each lesson in the study plan, have your child look at the questions in the printed book and answer them in the online answer sheet.

5. After completing all the lessons in the study plan, have your child take Practice Test 2.

6. View your child's performance by going to the *My Reports* section in the top right corner of the home page.

# Table of Contents

| | | |
|---|---|---|
| **Online Registration** | | 1 |
| **How to Use the Lumos Program** | | 2 |

| | | | |
|---|---|---|---|
| **Chapter 1** | **Reading Literature** | | 5 |
| Lesson 1 | Analysis of Key Events and Ideas | | 6 |
| Lesson 2 | Conclusions Drawn from the Text | | 14 |
| Lesson 3 | Development of Ideas | | 22 |
| Lesson 4 | Summary of Text | | 30 |
| Lesson 5 | Characters Responses and Changes | | 37 |
| Lesson 6 | Figurative Words and Phrases | | 46 |
| Lesson 7 | Connotative Words and Phrases | | 49 |
| Lesson 8 | Meaning of Words and Phrases | | 53 |
| Lesson 9 | Develop Setting | | 58 |
| Lesson 10 | Author's Purpose in a Text | | 66 |
| Lesson 11 | Compare Author's Writing to Another | | 70 |

| | | | |
|---|---|---|---|
| **Chapter 2** | **Reading Informational Text** | | 73 |
| Lesson 1 | Cite Textual Evidence | | 74 |
| Lesson 2 | Central Idea of Text | | 79 |
| Lesson 3 | Analyze How People, Events, or Ideas are Presented in Text | | 83 |
| Lesson 4 | Determine Technical Meanings | | 89 |
| Lesson 5 | Structure of Text | | 92 |
| Lesson 6 | Determine Author's Point of View | | 96 |
| Lesson 7 | Evaluating Arguments in Text | | 101 |
| Lesson 8 | Compare/Contrast One Author's Presentation with Another | | 106 |

| Chapter 3 | Language | 111 |
|---|---|---|
| Lesson 1 | Correct subject-verb agreement | 112 |
| Lesson 2 | Correct Use of Adjectives and Adverbs | 115 |
| Lesson 3 | Recognize Pronouns | 118 |
| Lesson 4 | Recognize and Correct Shifts in Pronoun | 121 |
| Lesson 5 | Recognize and Correct Vague Pronouns | 124 |
| Lesson 6 | Recognize Variations in English | 127 |
| Lesson 7 | Demonstrate command of Capitalization | 130 |
| Lesson 8 | Demonstrate Command of Punctuation | 133 |
| Lesson 9 | Correct Spelling | 136 |
| Lesson 10 | Vary Sentences | 139 |
| Lesson 11 | Maintain Consistency in Style and Tone | 142 |
| Lesson 12 | Use Clues To Determine Multiple-meaning Words | 144 |
| Lesson 13 | Use Context Clues to Determine Word Meaning | 148 |
| Lesson 14 | Use Common Roots and Affixes | 152 |
| Lesson 15 | Consult Reference Materials | 155 |
| Lesson 16 | Determine the Meaning of a Word | 158 |
| Lesson 17 | Interpret Figures of Speech | 161 |
| Lesson 18 | Use Relationships to Better Understand Words | 164 |
| Lesson 19 | Distinguish Between Word Associations and Definitions | 168 |
| Lesson 20 | Use Grade Appropriate Words | 170 |

| | | |
|---|---|---|
| Copyright | | 174 |
| What if I buy more than one Lumos tedBook? | | 175 |

# Chapter 1
# Reading Literature

Do NOT write your answers in this book. To open the answer sheet, scan the QR code or visit *lumoslearning.com/a/6e001*

## Lesson 1: Analysis of Key Events and Ideas

### Question 1 is based on the paragraph below

As it poured outside, I settled down by the window to watch the rain. The green park opposite my house looked even more green and fresh than usual. Strong winds shook the branches of the tall trees. Some of the branches swayed so hard in the strong winds that I thought they would break.

1. Why is the author using such clear descriptions?

   Ⓐ just to say that it was raining hard
   Ⓑ creating imagery to show the reader what that moment was like
   Ⓒ to tell us that the wind was blowing
   Ⓓ to explain what the trees look like when it rains

### Question 2 and 3 are based on the poem below

## The Forest's Sentinel

At night, when all is still
The forest's sentinel
Glides silently across the hill
And perches in an old pine tree,
A friendly presence his!
No harm can come
From night bird on the prowl.
His cry is mellow,
Much softer than a peacock's call.
Why then this fear of owls
Calling in the night?
If men must speak,
Then owls must hoot-
They have the right.

On me it casts no spell:
Rather, it seems to cry,
"The night is good- all's well, all's well."

-- RUSKIN BOND

## 2. From what point of view is the above poem?

Ⓐ First person point of view - from the owl's perspective
Ⓑ 3rd person point of view - from an unknown bystander or the author
Ⓒ First person point of view - from another animal's perspective
Ⓓ None of the above

## 3. According to the above poem, when does the owl come out?

Ⓐ At night
Ⓑ At dawn
Ⓒ At dusk
Ⓓ At noon

**Question 4 and 5 are based on the story below**

**After reading the story, enter the details in the map below. This will help you to answer the questions that follow.**

Once upon a time, four boys lived in the countryside. One boy was very clever, but he did not like books. His name was Good Sense. The other boys were not very clever, but they read every book in the school. When they became grown men, they decided to go out into the world to earn their livelihood.

They left home and came to a forest where they halted for the night. When they woke up in the morning, they found the bones of a lion. Three of them, who had learned their books well at school, decided to make a lion out of the bones.

Good Sense told them, "A lion is a dangerous animal. It will kill us. Don't make a lion." But the three disregarded his advice and started making a lion. Good Sense was very clever. When his friends were busy making the lion, he climbed up a tree to save himself. No sooner had the three young men created the lion and gave it life, than it pounced upon them and ate them up. Good Sense climbed down the tree and went home very sadly.

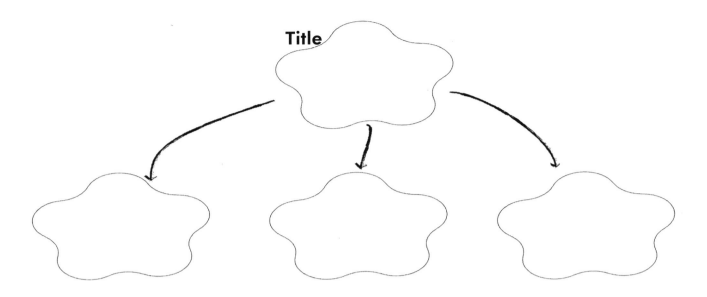

**Characters**  **Supporting Details**  **Main Idea**

4. **Part A**
   **What did they see in the forest when they woke up in the morning?**

   Ⓐ  the bones of a lion
   Ⓑ  a witch that could bring an animal to life
   Ⓒ  Good Sense hiding in a tree
   Ⓓ  none of the above

   **Part B**
   **What did the four friends decide when they became grown men?**

   Ⓐ  They decided to go out into the world and earn their livelihood.
   Ⓑ  They decided to play with animal bones.
   Ⓒ  They decided to be friends forever.
   Ⓓ  They decided to never leave home.

5. **What advice did Good Sense give his friends?**

   Ⓐ  He told them how to create the lion.
   Ⓑ  He told them how to beat the lion once it was created.
   Ⓒ  He told them not to create the lion.
   Ⓓ  He told them to hide from the lion once they created it.

### Question 6 is based on the story below

**After reading the story, enter the details in the map below. This will help you to answer the questions that follow.**

One evening, long after most people had gone to bed, a friend and I were making our way merrily back home through the silent and almost deserted streets. We had been to a musical show and were talking about the actor we had seen and heard in it.

"That show made him a star overnight," said my friend about one of the actors. "He was completely unknown before, and now thousands of teenagers send him chocolates and love letters through the mail."

"I thought he was quite good," I said, "but not worth thousands of love letters daily. As a matter of fact, one of his songs gave me pain."

"What was that?" my friend asked. "Sing to me." I burst into a parody of the song.

"Be quiet for heaven's sake!" My friend gave me an astonished look. "You'll give everybody a fright and wake people for miles around."

"Never mind," I said, intoxicated with the sound of my own voice. "I don't care. Why does it matter?"

And I went on singing the latest tunes at the top of my voice.

Suddenly, there came behind us the sound of heavy footsteps, and before I could say "Jack Robinson," a policeman was standing in front of me, his notebook open, and a determined look on his face.

"Excuse me, sir," he said. "You have a remarkable voice if I may say so. Who taught you to sing? I'd very much like to find someone who can give my daughter singing lessons. Would you be kind enough to tell me your name and address? Then my wife or I can drop you a line and discuss the matter."

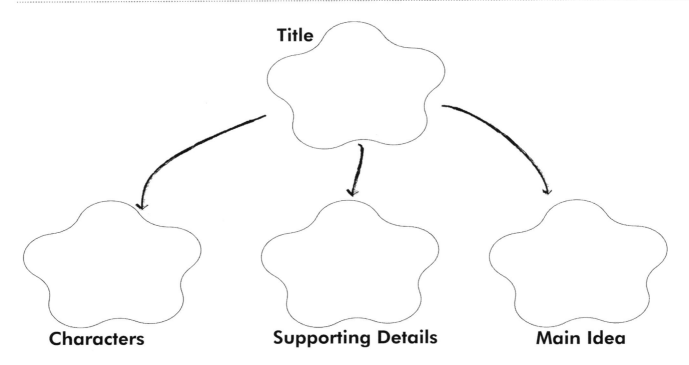

6. Why was the friend telling the singer to be quiet?

  Ⓐ  He did not like the sound of the singer's voice.
  Ⓑ  He was embarrassed.
  Ⓒ  He was worried that it would wake people for miles around.
  Ⓓ  Because the policeman told them to be quiet.

**Question 7 is based on the story below**

**After reading the story, enter the details in the map below. This will help you to answer the questions that follow.**

The sky was dark and overcast. It had been raining all night long, and there was no sign of it stopping. I thought that my Sunday would be ruined. As it poured outside, I settled down by the window to watch the rain. The park opposite my house looked even more green and fresh than usual. The branches of the tall trees swayed so hard in the strong wind that I thought they would break. A few children were splashing about in the mud puddles and having a wonderful time. I wished I could join them too! There were very few people out on the road and those who were hurried on their way, wrapped in raincoats and carrying umbrellas.

My mother announced that lunch was ready. It was piping hot and very welcoming in the damp weather. We spent the afternoon listening to music and to the downpour outside.

In the evening, we chatted and made paper boats that we meant to sail in the stream of water outside. It was not a bad day, after all!

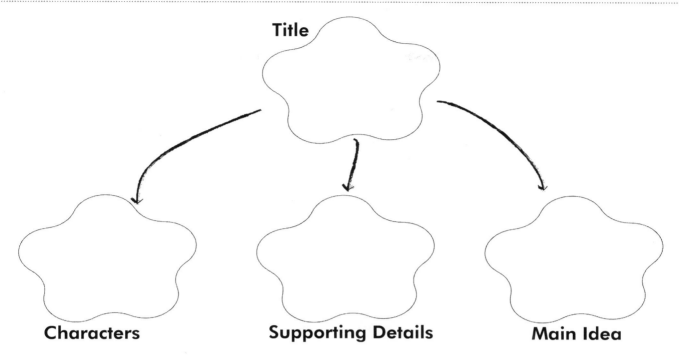

**7. What detail in the above passage tells us that the writer yearned to play outside?**

Ⓐ  The park opposite my house looked even more green and fresh.
Ⓑ  We spent the afternoon listening to music and to the downpour outside.
Ⓒ  I wished I could join them too!
Ⓓ  All of the above

**Question 8 is based on the poem below**

Faster than fairies, faster than witches,
Bridges and houses, hedges and ditches,
And charging along like troops in a battle,
All through the meadows the horses and cattle,
All of the sights of the hill and the plain,
Fly as thick as driving rain,
And ever again, in the wink of an eye,
Painted stations whistle by.

Here is a child who clambers and scrambles,
All by himself and gathering brambles;
Here is a tramp who stands and gazes,
And there is the green for stringing the daisies;
Here is a cart run away in the road,
Lumping along with man and load;

And here is a mill and there is a river,
Each a glimpse and gone forever.

-- R. L. STEVENSON

**8. What detail in the above poem tells us that this poem is about the view from inside a train?**

Ⓐ All of the sights of the hill and the plain, Fly as thick as driving rain
Ⓑ Faster than fairies, faster than witches, Bridges and houses, hedges and ditches,
Ⓒ And ever again, in the wink of an eye, Painted stations whistle by.
Ⓓ Here is a cart run away in the road

**Question 9 is based on the story below**

## Excerpt from Arabian Nights, Aladdin

After these words, the magician drew a ring off his finger, and put it on one of Aladdin's, telling him that it was a preservative against all evil, while he should observe what he had prescribed to him. After this instruction he said: "Go down boldly, child, and we shall both be rich all our lives."

Aladdin jumped into the cave, descended the steps, and found the three halls just as the African magician had described. He went through them with all the precaution the fear of death could inspire; crossed the garden without stopping, took down the lamp from the niche, threw out the wick and the liquor, and, as the magician had desired, put it in his vestband. But as he came down from the terrace, he stopped in the garden to observe the fruit, which he only had a glimpse of in crossing it. All the trees were loaded with extraordinary fruit, of different colors on each tree. Some bore fruit entirely white, and some clear and transparent as crystal; some pale red, and others deeper; some green, blue, and purple, and others yellow: in short, there were fruits of all colors. The white were pearls; the clear and transparent, diamonds; the deep red, rubies; the green, emeralds; the blue, turquoises; the purple, amethysts; and those that were of yellow cast, sapphires. Aladdin was altogether ignorant of their worth, and would have preferred figs and grapes, or any other fruits. But though he took them only for colored glass of little value, yet he was so pleased with the variety of the colors, and the beauty and extraordinary size of the seeming fruit, that he resolved to gather some of every sort; and accordingly filled the two new purses his uncle had bought for him with his clothes. Some he wrapped up in the skirts of his vest, which was of silk, large and full, and he crammed his bosom as full as it could hold.

Aladdin, having thus loaded himself with riches, returned through the three halls with the same precaution, made all the haste he could, that he might not make his uncle wait, and soon arrived at the mouth of the cave, where the African magician expected him with the utmost impatience. As soon as Aladdin saw him, he cried out: "Pray, uncle, lend me your hand, to help me out." "Give me the lamp first," replied the magician; "it will be troublesome to you." "Indeed, uncle," answered Aladdin, "I cannot now; it is not troublesome to me: but I will as soon as I am up." The African magician was so obstinate, that he would have the lamp before he would help him up; and Aladdin, who had encumbered himself so much with his fruit that he could not well get at it, refused to give it to him till he was out of the cave. The African magician, provoked at this obstinate refusal, flew into a passion, threw a little of his incense into the fire, which he had taken care to keep in, and no sooner pronounced two magical words, than the stone which had closed the mouth of the cave moved into its place, with the earth over it in the same manner as it lay at the arrival of the magician and Aladdin.

**9. What did the magician put on one of Aladdin's fingers? Write your answer in the box below.**

Do NOT write your answers in this book. To open the answer sheet, scan the QR code or visit **lumoslearning.com/a/6e002**

# Chapter 1 → Lesson 2: Conclusions Drawn from the Text

**Question 1 and 2 are based on the paragraph below**

**After reading the paragraph, enter the details in the map below. This will help you to answer the questions that follow.**

Sarah's mother told her to carry an umbrella on that Thursday morning before she left home for school, but Sarah did not want to do that. She already had her backpack and a gift for her friend to take with her. She just did not think it was necessary.

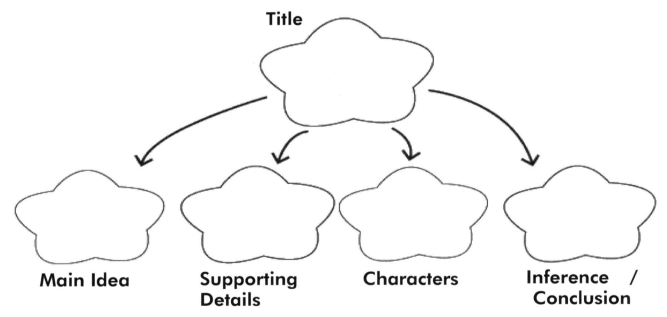

1. What can you infer about Sarah?

    Ⓐ   She is stubborn and only wants to do things if they seem right to her.
    Ⓑ   She does not like her mother.
    Ⓒ   She doesn't like getting wet.
    Ⓓ   She is a very obedient child.

2. What can you infer about the weather on that Thursday morning?

   Ⓐ It was raining.
   Ⓑ It was snowing.
   Ⓒ It was going to rain.
   Ⓓ It was a warm day.

**Question 3 is based on the paragraph below**

After reading the paragraph, enter the details in the map below. This will help you to answer the questions that follow.

The boy returned home a little late from school. He threw his coat as he walked in. He walked past his parents without greeting them. He headed straight to his room, slamming the door after him. He threw himself face down on his bed and lay there.

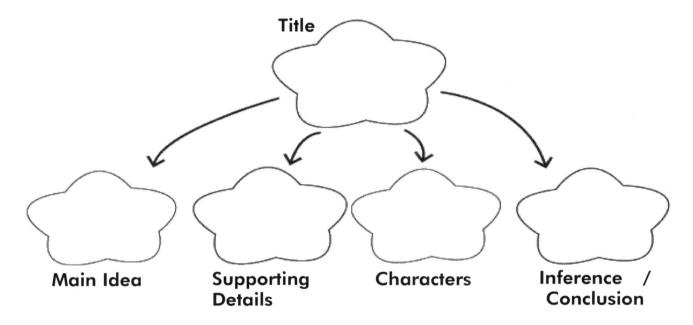

3. What do you believe the boy is experiencing in the passage?

   Ⓐ very delighted
   Ⓑ very disappointed
   Ⓒ very scared
   Ⓓ very excited

**4. Complete the sentence below.**

Katie called out to her mother. The aroma of freshly brewed coffee filled the air. The sizzling sound of frying eggs reached her ears as she glided down the stairs. Now she could smell toast and bacon too. She ran to the table and sank into her seat just as her mother walked in from the kitchen. She was ready for _____

Ⓐ Dinner
Ⓑ Lunch
Ⓒ Breakfast
Ⓓ Sleeping

**5. What is the most practical and ethical way for John to get candy now?**

John wanted to buy some candy at the store. When he got there he realized he forgot his money.

Ⓐ Ask the store owner if the candies can be given away for free.
Ⓑ Ask the people around you for money to buy candies.
Ⓒ Steal money from someone
Ⓓ Walk back home and get the money he forgot.

**Question 6 is based on the story below**

**After reading the story, enter the details in the map below. This will help you to answer the questions that follow.**

Once upon a time, four boys lived in the countryside. One boy was very clever, but he did not like books. His name was Good Sense. The other boys were not very clever, but they read every book in the school. When they became grown men, they decided to go out into the world to earn their livelihood.

They left home and came to a forest where they halted for the night. When they woke up in the morning, they found the bones of a lion. Three of them, who had learned their books well at school, decided to make a lion out of the bones.

Good Sense told them, "A lion is a dangerous animal. It will kill us. Don't make a lion." But the three disregarded his advice and started making a lion. Good Sense was very clever. When his friends were busy making the lion, he climbed up a tree to save himself. No sooner had the three young men created the lion and gave it life, than it pounced upon them and ate them up. Good Sense climbed down the tree and went home very sadly.

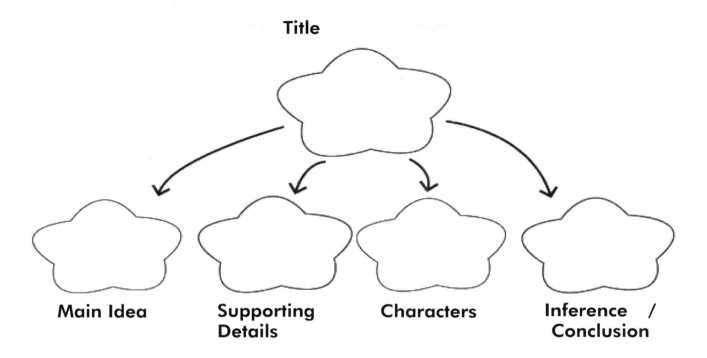

6. Which of the following statement(s) about Good Sense is/are true?

   Ⓐ He was very clever
   Ⓑ He did not like books
   Ⓒ He did not like the other boys
   Ⓓ Both A and B

7. We can infer that when people are doing sedentary activities, they must be _____.

   It is recommended that people should exercise every day, particularly those who spend many hours doing sedentary activities like playing cards, reading, or playing video games.

   Ⓐ Running
   Ⓑ Talking
   Ⓒ Sitting
   Ⓓ Jumping

### Question 8 is based on the story below

**After reading the story, enter the details in the map below. This will help you to answer the questions that follow.**

The sky was dark and overcast. It had been raining all night long, and there was no sign of it stopping. I thought that my Sunday would be ruined. As it poured outside, I settled down by the window to watch the rain. The park opposite my house looked even more green and fresh than usual. The branches of the tall trees swayed so hard in the strong wind that I thought they would break. A few children were splashing about in the mud puddles and having a wonderful time. I wished I could join them too! There were very few people out on the road and those who were hurried on their way, wrapped in raincoats and carrying umbrellas.

My mother announced that lunch was ready. It was piping hot and very welcoming in the damp weather. We spent the afternoon listening to music and to the downpour outside.

In the evening, we chatted and made paper boats that we meant to sail in the stream of water outside. It was not a bad day, after all!

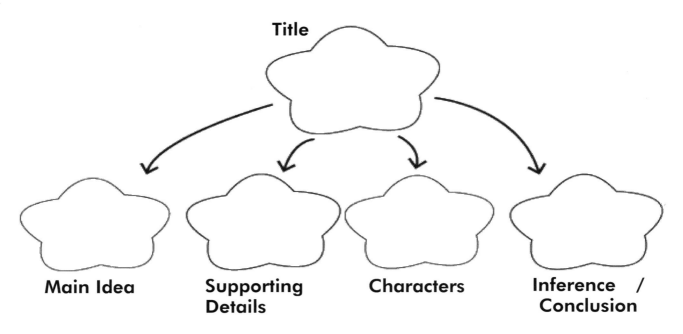

8. When did the event described in the passage occur?

   Ⓐ On a very nice and sunny day.
   Ⓑ On a wintry day.
   Ⓒ On a hot day.
   Ⓓ On a rainy day.

**Question 9 is based on the story below**

After reading the story, enter the details in the map below. This will help you to answer the questions that follow.

One evening, long after most people had gone to bed, a friend and I were making our way merrily back home through the silent and almost deserted streets. We had been to a musical show and were talking about the actor we had seen and heard in it.

"That show made him a star overnight," said my friend about one of the actors. "He was completely unknown before, and now thousands of teenagers send him chocolates and love letters through the mail."

"I thought he was quite good," I said, "but not worth thousands of love letters daily. As a matter of fact, one of his songs gave me pain."

"What was that?" my friend asked. "Sing to me." I burst into a parody of the song.

"Be quiet for heaven's sake!" My friend gave me an astonished look. "You'll give everybody a fright and wake people up for miles around."

"Never mind," I said, intoxicated with the sound of my own voice. "I don't care. How does it matter?"

And I went on singing the latest tunes at the top of my voice.

Presently there came behind us the sound of heavy footsteps, and before I could say "Jack Robinson," a policeman was standing in front of me, his notebook open, and a determined look on his face.

"Excuse me, sir," he said. "You have a remarkable voice if I may say so. Who taught you to sing? I'd very much like to find someone who can give my daughter singing lessons. Would you be kind enough to tell me your name and address? Then my wife or I can drop you a line and discuss the matter."

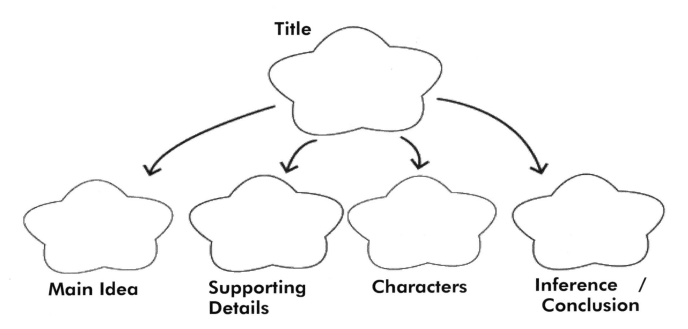

**9. Which detail in the above paragraph tells us that the author of the above passage is a male?**

Ⓐ "He was completely unknown before"
Ⓑ "And I went on singing the latest tunes at the top of my voice"
Ⓒ "Excuse me, sir," he said
Ⓓ "You have a remarkable voice"

**Question 10 is based on the passage below**

The boy and his dog were watching television when they heard a loud bang. There was a thunderstorm outside and the boy guessed that lightning must have hit something. The dog started to whimper and hid under the table.

You can guess that _____.

**10. Complete the sentence above.**

Ⓐ the dog was scared of the television show.
Ⓑ the dog was in trouble.
Ⓒ the dog was scared of the thunderstorm.
Ⓓ the dog needed to go outside.

11. What season is it?

The leaves were changing colors and there were pumpkins in people's yards.

☐

**Question 12 is based on the passage below**

Zoe is my dog, and she is white and brown. Zoe knows how to do a lot of tricks. Zoe can speak when you ask her to, and she can shake your hand. Zoe will also give you a kiss when you ask her. I don't know many dogs that can do these things.

12. What is the main idea of the passage?

Ⓐ Zoe is my dog.
Ⓑ Zoe can give kisses.
Ⓒ Zoe is smart.
Ⓓ Zoe only knows a few tricks.

**Question 13 is based on the passage below**

Jamie, please come home soon. I miss you when you are away and I am unhappy when you aren't here. I have missed your incredible cooking while you've been gone.

13. What is the main idea of the passage?

Ⓐ Jamie made the narrator unhappy.
Ⓑ Jamie is a good cook.
Ⓒ Jamie is away on vacation.
Ⓓ Jamie, I miss you.

Do NOT write your answers in this book. To open the answer sheet, scan the QR code or visit *lumoslearning.com/a/6e003*

# Chapter 1 → Lesson 3: Development of Ideas

### Question 1 is based on the passage below

I always try to do what I have promised to do. If I say I will arrive at 5:15, I try to be there at 5:15. I don't lie or deliberately withhold information. I don't try to trick or confuse others. My friends trust me with their secrets, and I don't tell them to anyone else. I understand that you are looking for a trustworthy employee.

**1. Select the concluding sentence that most completely summarizes the argument in the passage.**

   Ⓐ  If you are looking for an employee who doesn't lie, then you should hire me.
   Ⓑ  If you are looking for an employee who needs to be at work at 5:15, then you should hire me.
   Ⓒ  If you are looking for a trustworthy person, you should hire me.
   Ⓓ  I believe I would make a very good employee and would love to be considered for a position at your company.

### Question 2 is based on the passage below

If I am chosen to be class president, I will represent you on the Student Council. I will listen to your requests and be sure that they are heard. I will show up for meetings. I will try to make our school a better place.

**2. Select the concluding sentence that most completely summarizes the argument in the passage.**

   Ⓐ  If you vote for me, I will be a good class president.
   Ⓑ  I am a good leader.
   Ⓒ  I will work towards scrapping exams.
   Ⓓ  The food in the cafeteria is awful.

**Question 3 is based on the passage below**

Cats do not require as much attention as dogs. Dogs love you, and they want you to love them back. Cats are independent creatures. They don't need to be petted all the time. If you go on vacation for a few days, your dog may get lonely and refuse to eat, but your cat won't care.

3. Select the concluding sentence that most completely summarizes the argument in the passage.

    Ⓐ If you really want a pet, it would be a good idea to get a cat and a dog.
    Ⓑ If you don't have a lot of time to care for a pet, a dog is a better choice for you than a cat.
    Ⓒ Vacations are a good idea if you have a cat as a pet.
    Ⓓ If you don't have a lot of time to care for a pet, a cat is a better choice for you than a dog.

4. Choose the best possible supporting detail to most accurately complete the statements.

1. The beach is a perfect place to take a vacation.
2. I love to laze around on the sands.
3. _____
4. That is why I love to take a vacation at the beach.

    Ⓐ I love the smell of sea water.
    Ⓑ I hate the smell of sea water.
    Ⓒ Starfish are so cool.
    Ⓓ I like to see aircraft fly.

5. Choose the best possible supporting detail to most accurately complete the statements.

1. Christmas is everybody's favorite holiday.
2. One gets to do a lot of shopping.
3. _____.
4. That is why everybody loves Christmas.

    Ⓐ Christmas break is boring because you don't get to see your school friends every day.
    Ⓑ The school gives a lot of homework to do over the holidays.
    Ⓒ Decorating the Christmas tree is a lot of work.
    Ⓓ There's a spirit of giving.

### Question 6 is based on the story below

**After reading the story, enter the details in the map below. This will help you to answer the questions that follow.**

One evening, long after most people had gone to bed, a friend and I were making our way merrily back home through the silent and almost deserted streets. We had been to a musical show and were talking about the actor we had seen and heard in it.

"That show made him a star overnight," said my friend about one of the actors. "He was completely unknown before, and now thousands of teenagers send him chocolates and love letters through the mail."

"I thought he was quite good," I said, "but not worth thousands of love letters daily. As a matter of fact, one of his songs gave me pain."
"Which was that?" my friend asked. "Sing to me." I burst into a parody of the song.

"Be quiet for heaven's sake!" My friend gave me an astonished look. "You'll give everybody a fright and wake people up for miles around." And I went on singing the latest tunes at the top of my voice. Presently there came behind us the sound of heavy footsteps, and before I could say "Jack Robinson," a policeman was standing in front of me, his notebook open, and a determined look on his face.

"Excuse me, sir," he said. "You have a remarkable voice if I may say so. Who taught you to sing? I'd very much like to find someone who can give my daughter singing lessons. Would you be kind enough to tell me your name and address? Then my wife or I can drop you a line and discuss the matte

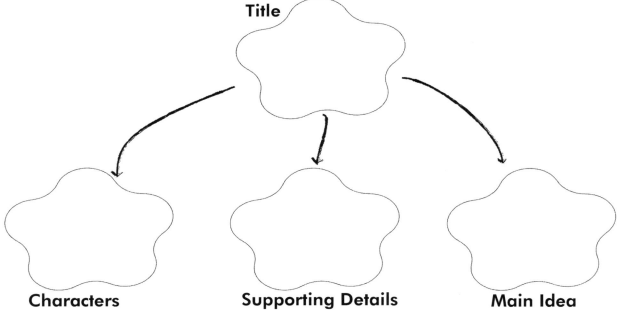

**6. Choose the best title for the above passage.**

Ⓐ The Singer
Ⓑ A Pleasant Surprise
Ⓒ The Musical Show
Ⓓ The Policeman

**Question 7 is based on the story below**

**After reading the story, enter the details in the map below. This will help you to answer the questions that follow.**

The sky was dark and overcast. It had been raining all night long, and there was no sign of it stopping. I thought that my Sunday would be ruined. As it poured outside, I settled down by the window to watch the rain. The park opposite my house looked even more green and fresh than usual. The branches of the tall trees swayed so hard in the strong wind that I thought they would break. A few children were splashing about in the mud puddles and having a wonderful time. I wished I could join them too! There were very few people out on the road and those who were hurried on their way, wrapped in raincoats and carrying umbrellas.

My mother announced that lunch was ready. It was piping hot and very welcoming in the damp weather. We spent the afternoon listening to music and to the downpour outside.

In the evening, we chatted and made paper boats that we meant to sail in the stream of water outside. It was not a bad day, after all!

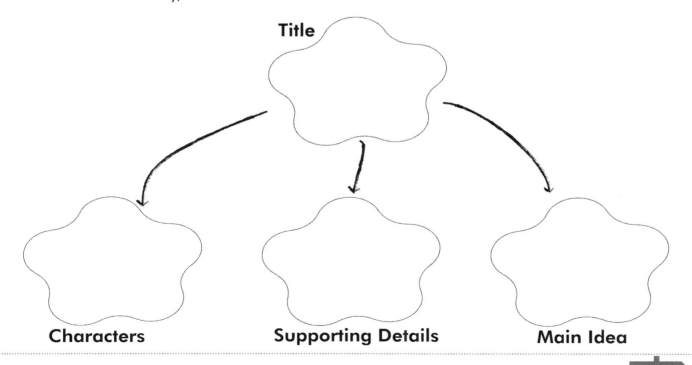

**7. What detail in the above passage tells us that it was a cloudy day?**

Ⓐ The sky was dark and overcast.
Ⓑ It had been raining all night long.
Ⓒ A few children were splashing about in the mud puddles.
Ⓓ The park opposite my house looked even more green and fresh.

### Question 8 is based on the paragraph below

The girls went to the park to play on the swings as they did each day. Their mothers always told them never to talk to strangers and always stick together. No one should walk home alone.

**8. What message did the girls get from their mothers?**

Ⓐ Stay together and stay away from strangers.
Ⓑ Only walk home alone if there is no one else to talk with you.
Ⓒ Be friendly to anyone you meet.
Ⓓ Enjoy the park and the people.

### Question 9 is based on the paragraph below

Suzanne and her brother always helped out at the shelter. They gave out food to people who would otherwise be hungry. They also gave out blankets, clothes, and jackets. Suzanne and her brother did this twice a month. When they gave these people food, blankets, clothes, and jackets, their faces lit up and they couldn't say thank you enough times.

**9. Which statement indicates the primary message?**

Ⓐ It is always nice and rewarding to help others.
Ⓑ Giving others blankets, clothes, and food can change their lives.
Ⓒ Giving people food will allow them to not go hungry.
Ⓓ Helping others always involves giving blankets.

### Question 10 is based on the paragraph below

Allison went to swim practice and worked very hard to try and perfect her flip turn. A flip turn is a turn where you flip underwater and turn to go back in the direction that you came from. Allison practiced 1 hour before school and 3 hours after school each day. On the weekends she practiced 5 hours a day! Allison thought she would never get the flip turn down right, but she practiced and practiced. Finally, after two weeks straight of practicing, she nailed it.

**10. Which statement indicates the primary message?**

Ⓐ  If you practice less than two weeks, you won't accomplish your goal.
Ⓑ  Only practice on the weekends.
Ⓒ  Keep trying and don't give up.
Ⓓ  Keep trying, but give up if you get too tired.

### Question 11 is based on the passage below

# Excerpt from Arabian Nights, Aladdin

**Read the below passage and answer the questions.**

After these words, the magician drew a ring off his finger, and put it on one of Aladdin's, telling him that it was a preservative against all evil, while he should observe what he had prescribed to him. After this instruction he said: "Go down boldly, child, and we shall both be rich all our lives."

Aladdin jumped into the cave, descended the steps, and found the three halls just as the African magician had described. He went through them with all the precaution the fear of death could inspire; crossed the garden without stopping, took down the lamp from the niche, threw out the wick and the liquor, and, as the magician had desired, put it in his vestband. But as he came down from the terrace, he stopped in the garden to observe the fruit, which he only had a glimpse of in crossing it. All the trees were loaded with extraordinary fruit, of different colors on each tree. Some bore fruit entirely white, and some clear and transparent as crystal; some pale red, and others deeper; some green, blue, and purple, and others yellow: in short, there were fruits of all colors. The white were pearls; the clear and transparent, diamonds; the deep red, rubies; the green, emeralds; the blue, turquoises; the purple, amethysts; and those that were of yellow cast, sapphires. Aladdin was altogether ignorant of their worth, and would have preferred figs and grapes, or any other fruits. But though he took them only for colored glass of little value, yet he was so pleased with the variety of the colors, and the beauty and extraordinary size of the seeming fruit, that he resolved to gather some of every sort; and accordingly filled the two new purses his uncle had bought for him with his clothes. Some he wrapped up in the skirts of his vest, which was of silk, large and full, and he crammed his bosom as full as it could hold.

Aladdin, having thus loaded himself with riches, returned through the three halls with the same precaution, made all the haste he could, that he might not make his uncle wait, and soon arrived at the mouth of the cave, where the African magician expected him with the utmost impatience. As soon as Aladdin saw him, he cried out: "Pray, uncle, lend me your hand, to help me out." "Give me the lamp first," replied the magician; "it will be troublesome to you." "Indeed, uncle," answered Aladdin, "I cannot now; it is not troublesome to me: but I will as soon as I am up." The African magician was so obstinate, that he would have the lamp before he would help him up; and Aladdin, who had encumbered himself so much with his fruit that he could not well get at it, refused to give it to him till he was out of the cave. The African magician, provoked at this obstinate refusal, flew into a passion, threw a little of his incense into the fire, which he had taken care to keep in, and no sooner pronounced two magical words, than the stone which had closed the mouth of the cave moved into its place, with the earth over it in the same manner as it lay at the arrival of the magician and Aladdin.

**11. The ring was a _____ against all evil. Write your answer in the box below.**

## Writing Task 1

**12. Writing Situation: The park in your area has only one tennis court. It is always crowded and one has to wait at least two hours before getting a chance to play.**

**Writing Task: Write a persuasive letter to your mayor requesting more tennis courts in your area. In your letter, be sure to describe the situation and explain the reasons why you need more tennis courts.**

Do NOT write your answers in this book. To open the answer sheet, scan the QR code or visit **lumoslearning.com/a/6e004**

# Chapter 1 → Lesson 4: Summary of Text

**Question 1 is based on the story below**

**After reading the story, enter the details in the map below. This will help you to answer the questions that follow.**

One evening, long after most people had gone to bed, a friend and I were making our way merrily back home through the silent and almost deserted streets. We had been to a musical show and were talking about the actor we had seen and heard in it.
"That show made him a star overnight," said my friend about one of the actors. "He was completely unknown before, and now thousands of teenagers send him chocolates and love letters through the mail."

"I thought he was quite good," I said, "but not worth thousands of love letters daily. As a matter of fact, one of his songs gave me pain."
"What was that?" my friend asked. "Sing to me." I burst into a parody of the song.
"Be quiet for heaven's sake!" My friend gave me an astonished look. "You'll give everybody a fright and wake people up for miles around."

"Never mind," I said, intoxicated with the sound of my own voice. "I don't care. How does it matter?" And I went on singing the latest tunes at the top of my voice.
Presently there came behind us the sound of heavy footsteps, and before I could say "Jack Robinson," a policeman was standing in front of me, his notebook open, and a determined look on his face.

"Excuse me, sir," he said. "You have a remarkable voice if I may say so. Who taught you to sing? I'd very much like to find someone who can give my daughter singing lessons. Would you be kind enough to tell me your name and address? Then my wife or I can drop you a line and discuss the matter."

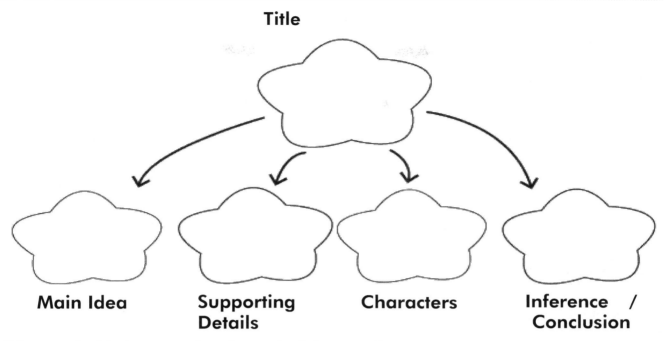

1. What probably happened at the end of the story?

   Ⓐ  Both the friends went home and had dinner
   Ⓑ  The writer gave the policeman his name and address.
   Ⓒ  The policeman arrested both the friends
   Ⓓ  They went to see another musical show

**Question 2 is based on the details below**

Thomas is on the football team, the basketball team, and the hockey team. He even likes to run when he has free time.

2. By reading this you can conclude that _____?

**Question 3 is based on the paragraph below**

Michael decided to climb a ladder to get his frisbee that landed on the roof. His father always told him to be careful when using a ladder because ladders were dangerous. Michael put on his bike helmet, asked his friend to hold the ladder, and put one hand in front of the other while climbing, never letting go of the ladder.

3. What can you conclude about climbing a ladder?

   Ⓐ It is a lot of fun.
   Ⓑ It is easy if you know what to do.
   Ⓒ You should only climb a ladder if you are over 13 years old.
   Ⓓ It can be very dangerous.

### Question 4 is based on the paragraph below

On the first day of school, there are many supplies that a student needs. Every student needs a notebook, pencils, pens, highlighters, and the most important, a calendar.

**4. What sentence below most closely agrees with these sentences?**

Ⓐ All of these items help a student stay organized throughout the year.
Ⓑ These items are only helpful for students who enjoy math.
Ⓒ These items are expensive, so only buy a few of them.
Ⓓ You may not need all these items to stay organized.

### Question 5 is based on the paragraph below

It is great to have a younger sibling. Some people may think it is annoying, but those people don't realize the benefits of having a younger sibling. First, a younger sibling can do your chores for you, so you don't get in trouble. Second, they can feed the animals, so you don't have to do that. Third, they can actually be fun to play with when you are stuck at home on a snow day.

**5. What can you summarize from this passage?**

Ⓐ It is great to have younger siblings.
Ⓑ Younger siblings are annoying.
Ⓒ You only want a sibling to be older than you.
Ⓓ Being an only child is the best.

### Question 6 is based on the paragraph below

Ryan earned money each week from doing chores around the house. His mother always told him that it was his money, but he should not spend it on useless things. Ryan decided to take $5.00 out of his piggy bank and went into the candy store. He looked at all the different types of candy and spent all of his $5.00.

**6. What is the most important message in this passage?**

Ⓐ Ryan loves candy.
Ⓑ Ryan begged for his money.
Ⓒ Ryan had a green piggy bank.
Ⓓ Ryan shared his candy with his friends.

**Question 7 is based on the paragraph below**

The little girl got to pick out new furniture and decorate her room. She really liked the white bed and dresser. She decided to paint her walls pink and get a pink carpet. She was so excited to be getting a new room!

**7. What can you summarize about this little girl?**

Ⓐ She had always had a room to herself.
Ⓑ She was excited to redo her room the way she wanted.
Ⓒ She wanted to paint her room purple.
Ⓓ Her mother wasn't happy with her decisions.

**Question 8 is based on the paragraph below**

Damon was moving to another state on the other side of the country. Along the way as his family drove, they stopped in Illinois, Idaho, and South Dakota; none of the towns they stopped in were like his hometown. When he arrived in his new hometown, he was excited to be living in a different state.

**8. What can you summarize about this passage?**

Ⓐ Damon was moving to South Dakota.
Ⓑ Damon guessed that his new hometown would not be like his old hometown, but was excited to be moving anyway.
Ⓒ Damon did not want to stop in other states along the way.
Ⓓ Damon was moving to Illinois.

**Question 9 is based on the poem below**

The girl stood looking out the window
No one was out there, not even an animal.
The wind blew softly and rain started to fall.
The clouds rolled in and the thunder came.
The girl felt like she was looking through the window into her own mood.

**9. Based on this poem, what answer best describes the girl's mood?**

Ⓐ The girl liked to be alone.
Ⓑ She was scared of the rain.
Ⓒ The girl was sad and unhappy.
Ⓓ The girl was excited.

### Question 10 is based on the poem below

A boy embarked on a journey
Not knowing where he would end up.
He packed his things and headed out West.
It took him days and days to get to where he was going.
He was nervous and scared about what may be out there.
When the boy arrived, he wasn't sure if he was ready for what was to come.

**10. What was the boy doing?**

Ⓐ The boy was moving and starting a new life.
Ⓑ The boy was going to become an actor.
Ⓒ The boy was going to find his long lost brother.
Ⓓ The boy was going on a vacation.

### Question 11 is based on the story below

**After reading the story, enter the details in the map below. This will help you to answer the questions that follow.**

Once upon a time, four boys lived in the countryside. One boy was very clever, but he did not like books. His name was Good Sense. The other boys were not very clever, but they read every book in the school. When they became grown men, they decided to go out into the world to earn their livelihood.

They left home and came to a forest where they halted for the night. When they woke up in the morning, they found the bones of a lion. Three of them, who had learned their books well at school, decided to make a lion out of the bones.

Good Sense told them, "A lion is a dangerous animal. It will kill us. Don't make a lion." But the three disregarded his advice and started making a lion. Good Sense was very clever. When his friends were busy making the lion, he climbed up a tree to save himself. No sooner had the three young men created the lion and gave it life, than it pounced upon them and ate them up. Good Sense climbed down the tree and went home very sadly.

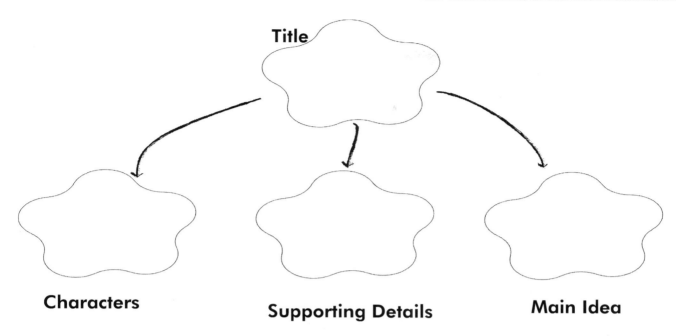

11. Part A
    What can be an appropriate title for the above story?

    Ⓐ The Four Friends
    Ⓑ Good Sense
    Ⓒ The Lion and the Friends
    Ⓓ The Men

    Part B
    What is the moral of the story?

    Ⓐ Listen to a wise person's advice
    Ⓑ Never listen to someone who does not like to read books
    Ⓒ Think before you act
    Ⓓ Both A and C

**Question 12 is based on the poem below**

I'm nobody! Who are you?

I'm nobody! Who are you?
Are you nobody, too?
Then there's a pair of us — don't tell!
They'd banish us; you know!

How dreary to be somebody!
How public like a frog
To tell one's name the livelong day
To an admiring bog!

-Emily Dickinson

Emily Dickinson is a well- known American poet who was born in the 1800's.

**12. What do you think she is talking about in this poem?**

- Ⓐ She feels as if people do not see or notice her, and she likes it that way.
- Ⓑ She wants to be a frog.
- Ⓒ She doesn't like being not noticed and does want to be important.
- Ⓓ She is not making any comparisons in this poem.

## Chapter 1 → Lesson 5: Characters Responses and Changes

**Question 1 and 2 are based on the story below**

**After reading the story, enter the details in the map below. This will help you to answer the questions that follow.**

One evening, long after most people had gone to bed, a friend and I were making our way merrily back home through the silent and almost deserted streets. We had been to a musical show and were talking about the actor we had seen and heard in it.

"That show made him a star overnight," said my friend about one of the actors. "He was completely unknown before, and now thousands of teenagers send him chocolates and love letters through the mail."

"I thought he was quite good," I said, "but not worth thousands of love letters daily. As a matter of fact, one of his songs gave me pain."

"Which was that?" my friend asked. "Sing to me." I burst into a parody of the song.
"Be quiet for heaven's sake!" My friend gave me an astonished look. "You'll give everybody a fright and wake people up for miles around."
"Never mind," I said, intoxicated with the sound of my own voice. "I don't care. Why does it matter?"

And I went on singing the latest tunes at the top of my voice. Presently there came behind us the sound of heavy footsteps, and before I could say "Jack Robinson," a policeman was standing in front of me, his notebook open, and a determined look on his face.

"Excuse me, sir," he said. "You have a remarkable voice if I may say so. Who taught you to sing? I'd very much like to find someone who can give my daughter singing lessons. Would you be kind enough to tell me your name and address? Then my wife or I can drop you a line and discuss the matter."

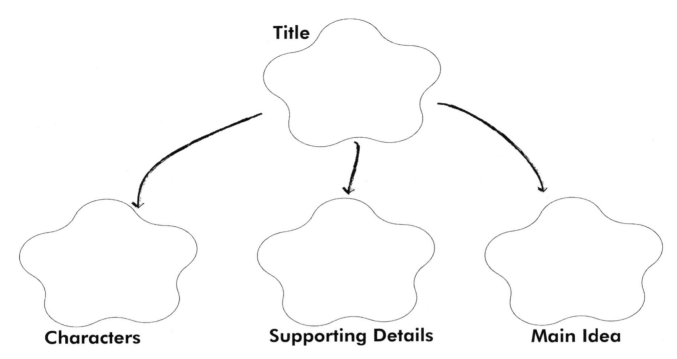

1. Who are the three characters in the above passage?

   Ⓐ  the writer, the writer's friend, and the actor
   Ⓑ  the writer, the writer's friend, and the singer
   Ⓒ  the neighbors, the policeman, and his friend
   Ⓓ  the writer, the writer's friend, and the policeman

2. Who were the writer and his friend referring to when they were talking and said "his songs"?

   Ⓐ  their neighbors
   Ⓑ  the policeman
   Ⓒ  the actor who sang in the musical show
   Ⓓ  the friend

### Question 3 and 4 are based on the story below

**After reading the story, enter the details in the map below. This will help you to answer the questions that follow.**

The sky was dark and overcast. It had been raining all night long, and there was no sign of it stopping. I thought that my Sunday would be ruined. As it poured outside, I settled down by the window to watch the rain. The park opposite my house looked even more green and fresh than usual. The branches of the tall trees swayed so hard in the strong wind that I thought they would break. A few children were splashing about in the mud puddles and having a wonderful time. I wished I could join them too! There were very few people out on the road and those who were hurried on their way, wrapped in raincoats and carrying umbrellas.

My mother announced that lunch was ready. It was piping hot and very welcoming in the damp weather. We spent the afternoon listening to music and to the downpour outside.

In the evening, we chatted and made paper boats that we meant to sail in the stream of water outside. It was not a bad day, after all!

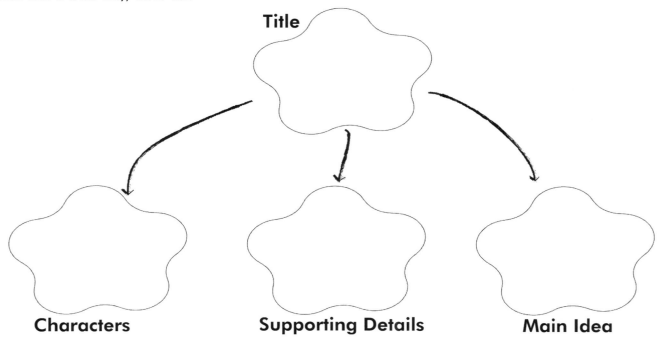

3. Who is the main character in the above passage?

   Ⓐ  The rain
   Ⓑ  The writer's mom
   Ⓒ  The writer
   Ⓓ  The wind

**4. The character in a story who dominates is a _____.**

Ⓐ  minor character
Ⓑ  major character
Ⓒ  supporting character
Ⓓ  Joker

**Question 5 and 6 are based on the story below**

**After reading the story, enter the details in the map below. This will help you to answer the questions that follow.**

Sally woke up earlier than she expected one morning. Something wasn't right. She then realized what had awakened her. It was an unfamiliar sound. She listened closely and realized that the sound was coming from outside. Climbing out of her bed, she slipped into her robe and slippers and went to the window. Looking out, she soon spotted a small kitten under the tree that stood outside her window. She stood, staring at the helpless creature. It didn't move. It soon spotted her and meowed, as if it were calling out to her.

Sally left her room and found her mother in the kitchen. She excitedly told her mom about the kitten. "I am going outside to get the poor little thing," she told her mother.

"I'll go with you," her mom replied. Together they walked into the backyard. The kitten was still there waiting for them. Sally picked it up in her arms. The little kitten felt so soft and cuddly. She had always wanted a kitten and wondered if her mother would allow her to keep him. Her mother decided to first feed the kitten. She also decided to make a few calls to see where he came from. The kitten certainly needed a home. Sally became more hopeful that she would be able to keep the kitten.

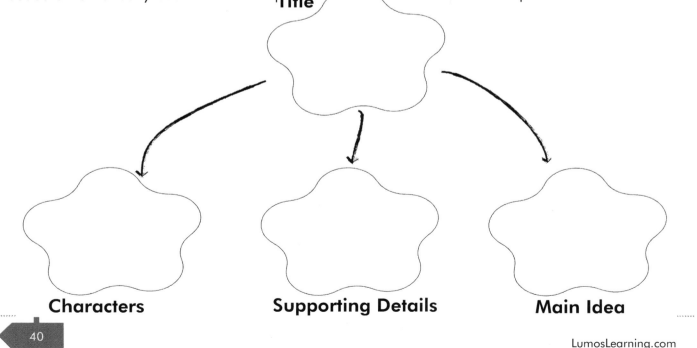

**5. The characters in the story are _____.**

Ⓐ the kitten
Ⓑ the mother
Ⓒ Sally
Ⓓ All of the above

**6. The main character in a story is usually known as the _____.**

Ⓐ Protagonist
Ⓑ Antagonist
Ⓒ One who saves everyone
Ⓓ The one who messes everything up

**7. The descriptions given by an author about the character's personality, habits, likes and dislikes are called?**

Ⓐ Character style
Ⓑ Character flaws
Ⓒ Character traits
Ⓓ Character ideas

> **Question 8 is based on the sentence below**

Having to start at a new school didn't worry Jane at all; she was ready for anything.

**8. A character trait of Jane is _____.**

Ⓐ Easy-going
Ⓑ Shy
Ⓒ Scared
Ⓓ Nervous

### Question 9 is based on the sentence below

Realizing his son's dog was still in the burning building, the dad ran back into the building.

**9. A character trait of the father is _____.**

- Ⓐ Nervous
- Ⓑ Scared
- Ⓒ Carefree
- Ⓓ Selfless

### Question 10 is based on the sentences below

Ever since Greg was little, he always liked to take things apart. He took apart his sister's dolls, took apart all his trucks and cars, and even took apart his parents' telephone to see how it worked.

**10. Which character trait best describes Greg?**

- Ⓐ Destructive
- Ⓑ Angry
- Ⓒ Curious
- Ⓓ Mean

### Question 11 is based on the passage below

**Excerpt from Arabian Nights, Aladdin**

After these words, the magician drew a ring off his finger, and put it on one of Aladdin's, telling him that it was a preservative against all evil, while he should observe what he had prescribed to him. After this instruction he said: "Go down boldly, child, and we shall both be rich all our lives."

Aladdin jumped into the cave, descended the steps, and found the three halls just as the African magician had described. He went through them with all the precaution the fear of death could inspire; crossed the garden without stopping, took down the lamp from the niche, threw out the wick and the liquor, and, as the magician had desired, put it in his vestband. But as he came down from the terrace, he stopped in the garden to observe the fruit, which he only had a glimpse of in crossing it. All the trees were loaded with extraordinary fruit, of different colors on each tree. Some bore fruit entirely white, and some clear and transparent as crystal; some pale red, and others deeper; some green, blue, and purple, and others yellow: in short, there was fruit of all colors. The white were pearls; the clear and transparent, diamonds; the deep red, rubies; the green, emeralds; the blue, turquoises; the purple, amethysts; and those that were of yellow cast, sapphires. Aladdin was altogether ignorant of their worth, and would have preferred figs and grapes, or any other fruits. But though he took them only for coloured glass of little value, yet he was so pleased with the variety of the colors, and the beauty and extraordinary size of the seeming fruit, that he resolved to gather some of every sort; and accordingly filled the two new purses his uncle had bought for him with his clothes. Some he wrapped up in the skirts of his vest, which was of silk, large and full, and he crammed his bosom as full as it could hold.

Aladdin, having thus loaded himself with riches, returned through the three halls with the same precaution, made all the haste he could, that he might not make his uncle wait, and soon arrived at the mouth of the cave, where the African magician expected him with the utmost impatience. As soon as Aladdin saw him, he cried out: "Pray, uncle, lend me your hand, to help me out." "Give me the lamp first," replied the magician; "it will be troublesome to you." "Indeed, uncle," answered Aladdin, "I cannot now; it is not troublesome to me: but I will as soon as I am up." The African magician was so obstinate, that he would have the lamp before he would help him up; and Aladdin, who had encumbered himself so much with his fruit that he could not well get at it, refused to give it to him till he was out of the cave. The African magician, provoked at this obstinate refusal, flew into a passion, threw a little of his incense into the fire, which he had taken care to keep in, and no sooner pronounced two magical words, than the stone which had closed the mouth of the cave moved into its place, with the earth over it in the same manner as it lay at the arrival of the magician and Aladdin.

**11. Why did the magician get angry with Aladdin on his return? Write your answer in the box below.**

### Question 12 is based on the sentences below

**Increase Your Vocabulary**

**Additional vocabulary to add:**

**Caveat emptor-** [**kav**-ee-ah**temp**-tawr] Latin, noun, let the buyer beware. The person who is purchasing something is responsible for noting any problems with their purchase, unless a warranty is made.

**Carte blanche-** [kart blahnSH] French, noun, complete freedom to act as one wishes thinks is best. Full discretionary power.

**Tete a tete-** [ 2 is also] French, noun, a personal conversation between two people. Adjective, face to face, private. Adverb, in private.

**Alfresco-** []   Italian,  adj, adv, open air, outdoors.

**Pas de deaux** - [pa de du] French, noun, a dance duet in which 2 dancers perform ballet steps.

**Bon appetite** - [bawna-pey-tee] French, true meaning is that may you enjoy your meal; however, in France it is a saying that the host announces to let the guests know it is time to begin eating.

**Quid pro quo** - [kwid]  Latin, noun, something given or received for something else.

**Alma mater-**  Latin, noun, an institution, school, university, college, where one has graduated from.

Practice questions and explanations.

In the English language, numerous words are derived from other languages and used frequently in written English. These words have become common place to most people.  However, some may be unfamiliar and it is necessary to describe their origin for greater understanding of their meaning.

**Sample sentences to reinforce understanding of derived meanings:**

When purchasing a couch at the antique auction, Mr Willis took note of caveat emptor before agreeing to the sale.

We had carte blanche when it came to choosing our fishing site, guide, and schooner at the hotel in the Caribbean.

It was obvious that the couple was engaged in a tete a tete as they huddled in the corner booth.

The group enjoyed their time dining <u>alfresco</u> on the San Antonio River Walk in San Antonio, Texas.

The dancers had perfected the <u>pas de deaux</u> while performing Sleeping Beauty at the local theatre.

As usual, Maryann announced "<u>Bon appetite</u>" as we began our first-course appetizers at the French restaurant.

It was obvious to all who attended the hearing that <u>quid pro quo</u> was applicable in the case in front of the jury.

Scott and Sarah were boisterous and could be heard above the entire crowd as they sang during their 20th-year reunion at their <u>alma mater</u> in Dayton, Ohio.

**12. Look at the words given below.**

1. graduated from
2. a private meeting between 2 people
3. dance step with 2 people
4. contract made between parties for services
5. full discretionary power
6. salutation to eat
7. outside
8. buyer beware

**Match the following vocabulary with its meaning from the list of words given above.**

| Alma mater | ———— | |
| Pas de deaux | ———— | |
| Carte blanche | ———— | |
| Bon appetite | ———— | |
| Tete a tete | ———— | |
| Quid pro quo | ———— | |
| Alfresco | ———— | |
| Caveat emptor | ———— | |

Do NOT write your answers in this book. To open the answer sheet, scan the QR code or visit **lumoslearning.com/a/6e006**

## Chapter 1 → Lesson 6: Figurative Words and Phrases

1. **Choose the sentence below that is closest in meaning to the figurative expression.**

   Edgar was dead to the world when we got home.

   Ⓐ  Edgar was asleep when we got home.
   Ⓑ  Edgar was not moving or breathing.
   Ⓒ  Edgar had a head injury and was unconscious.
   Ⓓ  Edgar was not at home.

2. **Choose the sentence below that is closest in meaning to the figurative expression.**

   You'd better go home; you're in hot water.

   Ⓐ  You'd better go home; you're in trouble
   Ⓑ  You'd better go home; you'll find hot water there.
   Ⓒ  You'd better go home; you are sweating.
   Ⓓ  You'd better go home and drink hot water.

3. **Choose the sentence below that is closest in meaning to the figurative expression.**

   He put all the papers in the circular file.

   Ⓐ  He put the papers in the wastebasket.
   Ⓑ  He rolled up all the papers.
   Ⓒ  He put the papers in the round file cabinet.
   Ⓓ  He put the papers on the circular table.

**4. Choose the word below that, completes the figurative expression.**

He works like a _____.

Ⓐ Lion
Ⓑ Dog
Ⓒ Parrot
Ⓓ Cat

**5. Choose the word below that, completes the figurative expression.**

He is as stubborn as a _____.

Ⓐ Mule
Ⓑ Cow
Ⓒ Baby
Ⓓ Ice

**6. Choose the sentence below that is closest in meaning to the figurative expression.**

The secretary had a mountain of paper work. _____.

Ⓐ The secretary was dealing with paper art
Ⓑ The secretary had a large amount of work
Ⓒ The secretary had to run around a lot
Ⓓ The secretary had to meet a lot of people

**7. Complete the sentence below so that it is closest in meaning to the figurative expression.**

His room is a train wreck. It is _____.

Ⓐ full of toy trains
Ⓑ well organized
Ⓒ a mess
Ⓓ well laid out

**8. Complete the sentence below so that it is closest in meaning to the figurative expression.**

He is a star. He _____.

Ⓐ he loves soccer
Ⓑ wants to be an astronomer
Ⓒ acts in films
Ⓓ is very good at what he does

**9. Complete the sentence below so that it is closest in meaning to the figurative expression.**

She is my rock. She always _____ me.

Ⓐ puts me down
Ⓑ leans on
Ⓒ criticizes
Ⓓ supports

**10. Complete the sentence below so that it is closest in meaning to the figurative expression.**

I feel like a million bucks. I am _____.

Ⓐ elated
Ⓑ happy
Ⓒ discontented
Ⓓ Both A & B

**11. Choose the sentence below that is closest in meaning to the figurative expression.**

He put his foot in his mouth.

Ⓐ He said something funny.
Ⓑ He said something difficult to understand.
Ⓒ He was sarcastic.
Ⓓ He said something he regretted.

**12. Choose the sentence below that is closest in meaning to the figurative expression.**

Don't bug me!

Ⓐ Don't bother me.
Ⓑ Don't sneak.
Ⓒ Don't tell me anything about yourself.
Ⓓ Don't try to get the better of me.

**13. Choose the sentence below that is closest in meaning to the figurative expression.**

He quit smoking cold turkey.

Ⓐ He quit eating poultry.
Ⓑ He quit cooking.
Ⓒ He quit smoking suddenly and without help.
Ⓓ He quit smoking Turkish cigars.

Do NOT write your answers in this book. To open the answer sheet, scan the QR code or visit *lumoslearning.com/a/6e007*

# Chapter 1 → Lesson 7: Connotative Words and Phrases

1. **Choose the best word to complete each sentence.**

    My friend is very careful about spending money. I admire that, so I call him _____.

    Ⓐ thrifty
    Ⓑ stingy
    Ⓒ miserly
    Ⓓ selfish

2. **Choose the best word to complete each sentence.**

    My friend is very careful about spending money. I don't like that trait, so I call him _____

    Ⓐ thrifty
    Ⓑ stingy
    Ⓒ rude
    Ⓓ mean

3. **Choose the best word to complete each sentence.**

    I admire the man who jumped on the subway tracks to rescue a stranger. He was certainly _____.

    Ⓐ foolhardy
    Ⓑ undecided
    Ⓒ courageous
    Ⓓ stupid

**Question 4 is based on the poem below**

Faster than fairies, faster than witches,
Bridges and houses, hedges and ditches,
And charging along like troops in a battle,
All through the meadows the horses and cattle,
All of the sights of the hill and the plain,
Fly as thick as driving rain,
And ever again, in the wink of an eye,
Painted stations whistle by.

Here is a child who clambers and scrambles,
All by himself and gathering brambles;
Here is a tramp who stands and gazes,
And there is the green for stringing the daisies;
Here is a cart run away in the road,
Lumping along with man and load;
And here is a mill and there is a river,
Each a glimpse and gone forever.

-- R. L. STEVENSON

**4. In the above poem what does the word "brambles" mean?**

Ⓐ people
Ⓑ crowds of people
Ⓒ train stations
Ⓓ prickly blueberry - and blackberry bushes

**Question 5 is based on the passage below**

The girls on the playground were playing hopscotch. They all played together at recess every day. The new girl sat at the corner of the playground by herself, so one of the girls was _____ and asked her if she wanted to join them.

**5. Which word best completes the sentence?**

Ⓐ Snotty
Ⓑ Proud
Ⓒ Friendly
Ⓓ Clever

**Question 6 is based on the sentence below**

Micky and Janie live in a quiet neighborhood and are very sweet and polite. However, the husband and wife are upset by their noisy neighbors.

**6. Which of the following represents what they might say to their neighbors?**

Ⓐ Hey! Keep quiet over there!
Ⓑ Hello...would you mind keep the noise level down? We have sleeping children over here.
Ⓒ How dare you make this much noise when we have sleeping children over here!
Ⓓ If you don't get quiet in the next 5 minutes, we're calling the cops!

**7. Which word best completes the sentence?**

The first aid supplies that were brought after the hurricane were _____. Even after they came, the survivors of the hurricane kept looking for supplies.

Ⓐ inadequate
Ⓑ helpful
Ⓒ tragic
Ⓓ important

**8. What word best fits in the blank?**

Skipping school can _____ your future.

Ⓐ effect
Ⓑ help
Ⓒ affect
Ⓓ None of the above

**9. What word best fits in the blank?**

The _____ candidate put his hands high in the sky and pumped his arms with a huge smile on his face.

Ⓐ unhappy
Ⓑ bewildered
Ⓒ victorious
Ⓓ fun

**10. What word best fits in the blank?**

Jackie read the newspaper and found out that there was a twister that hit Alabama and her heart broke for the affected families. The twister wiped out hundreds of houses. This was such a _____ event.

Ⓐ exciting
Ⓑ tragic
Ⓒ unimportant
Ⓓ victorious

**11. What word describes this girl's behavior?**

The little girl threw her dolls all over her room, took her crayons and drew on the wall of her bedroom, and even pulled the dog's tail.

Ⓐ snotty
Ⓑ bratty
Ⓒ nervous
Ⓓ happy

# Chapter 1 → Lesson 8: Meaning of Words and Phrases

**Question 1 is based on the paragraph below**

"That show made him a star overnight", said my friend about one of the actors. "He was completely unknown before. And now thousands of teenagers send him chocolates and love letters in the mail."

1. What does the above paragraph mean?

    Ⓐ that the actor had poor acting skills
    Ⓑ that the actor had come to fame recently
    Ⓒ that nobody likes him now
    Ⓓ none of the above

**Question 2 and 3 are based on the poem below**

The forest's sentinel
Glides silently across the hill
And perches in an old pine tree,
A friendly presence his!
No harm can come
From night bird on the prowl.
His cry is mellow,
Much softer than a peacock's call.

Why then this fear of owls
Calling in the night?
If men must speak,
Then owls must hoot-
They have the right.
On me it casts no spell:
Rather, it seems to cry,
"The night is good- all's well, all's well."

-- RUSKIN BOND

**2. What is the poet talking about in the first stanza?**

Ⓐ how the owl comes out into the night
Ⓑ how the owl catches its prey
Ⓒ how the owl is looking into the dark night
Ⓓ how the owl walks

**3. What is the poet saying about the owl?**

Ⓐ He is comparing the owl to a sentinel
Ⓑ He is describing the flight of the owl
Ⓒ He is saying that the owl is friendly and harmless
Ⓓ All of the above

The sky was dark and overcast. It had been raining all night long, and there was no sign of it stopping. I thought that my Sunday would be ruined. As it poured outside, I settled down by the window to watch the rain. The park opposite my house looked even more green and fresh than usual. The branches of the tall trees swayed so hard in the strong wind that I thought they would break. A few children were splashing about in the mud puddles and having a wonderful time. I wished I could join them too! There were very few people out on the road and those who were hurried on their way, wrapped in raincoats and carrying umbrellas.

My mother announced that lunch was ready. It was piping hot and very welcoming in the damp weather. We spent the afternoon listening to music and to the downpour outside.

In the evening, we chatted and made paper boats that we meant to sail in the stream of water outside. It was not a bad day, after all!

**4. How does the writer end the passage?**

Ⓐ With a satisfied tone
Ⓑ With a sad tone
Ⓒ With an annoyed tone
Ⓓ With an excited tone

### Question 5 is based on the paragraph below

Androcles was a slave who escaped from his master and fled to the forest. As he was wandering there, he came upon a lion lying down moaning and groaning. Seeing the lion in pain, he removed a huge thorn from the beast's paw. After this incident, they lived together as great friends in the forest. Androcles was eventually arrested and condemned to death in the arena. He would be thrown to a lion that was captured and not given food for several days. The Emperor and his courtiers came to see the spectacle. Androcles was lead to the middle of the arena and so was the hungry lion. The lion roared and rushed towards its victim. But, as soon as he came near Androcles, he recognized him and licked his hands like a friendly dog. Everyone was surprised. The emperor heard the whole story and pardoned Androcles and freed the lion to his native forest.

5. This story brings out the meaning of _____.

   Ⓐ  Friendship
   Ⓑ  Slavery
   Ⓒ  Escape
   Ⓓ  Hunger

### Question 6 is based on the paragraph below

Last week, I fell off my bike and hurt myself badly. I bruised my elbow and sprained my wrist. My injuries would have been worse if I hadn't been wearing my bicycle helmet. My doctor asked me to tell this to all my friends so that they would wear helmets too. I told my teacher, and she asked me to make a public announcement during the school assembly. I had to talk about the accident and how the helmet protected me.

6. Why was I asked to tell everyone about my accident and mention wearing the helmet?

   Ⓐ  so that everyone understands the benefit of wearing a helmet
   Ⓑ  because it made an interesting story
   Ⓒ  so that everyone comes to know what a hero I am
   Ⓓ  so that helmets can be sold

7. What is the mood of this sentence?

   Life and death were ideal as they crept into the dark world.

   Ⓐ  Ominous
   Ⓑ  Tragic
   Ⓒ  Dramatic
   Ⓓ  Silly

## 8. What is the tone of this sentence?

The man was feeble-minded and did not realize when others made fun of him by laughing at him and talking behind his back.

Ⓐ Unconcerned
Ⓑ Upsetting
Ⓒ Angry
Ⓓ Rude

**Question 9 is based on the poem below**

My brother comes in my room and hides my dolls,
but my brother plays hide and seek with me.
My brother tells me I'm annoying and should leave his room,
but my brother stands up for me on the playground when someone is mean to me.
My brother plays with his friends and tells me I'm too young to join them,
but my brother plays with me in the snow when we have a snow day.

## 9. What is the hidden meaning in the poem?

Ⓐ The brother easily gets frustrated with his sibling.
Ⓑ The brother doesn't want to play with his sibling.
Ⓒ The brother really loves his sibling.
Ⓓ The brother likes to play with dolls.

**Question 10 is based on the poem below**

Without you here, I can move forward
Thinking of the past only makes it worse,
Forgetting is the only way to continue on

## 10. What is the meaning of the poem?

Ⓐ The narrator is angry at someone
Ⓑ The narrator is moving away
Ⓒ The narrator wants to think of all the memories
Ⓓ The narrator wants to move forward; it is too sad to look back

**Question 11 is based on the sentences below**

Joe went into school with his clothes on backwards. He even dyed his hair green. He brought a few magic tricks in and did them for his friends. When he did them, they all laughed.

**11. Based on these sentences, what inference can you make about Joe?**

- Ⓐ  Joe is serious.
- Ⓑ  Joe is rude.
- Ⓒ  Joe is funny.
- Ⓓ  Joe is caring.

**Question 12 is based on the passage below**

Samantha was on the track team and was trying to perform her personal best in the high jump. She jumped 4 feet and made it over with ease. She then attempted her personal best at 5 feet, but did not make it on her first attempt. She tried four more times and, on the fifth try, she made it!

**12. What is the meaning of this passage?**

- Ⓐ  Keep trying to perform your personal best even if you fail the first time.
- Ⓑ  Only try something five times.
- Ⓒ  If you fail to perform your personal best, you may not succeed, even if you try again.
- Ⓓ  The faster you run, the higher you can go.

Do NOT write your answers in this book. To open the answer sheet, scan the QR code or visit **lumoslearning.com/a/6e009**

# Chapter 1 → Lesson 9: Develop Setting

**Question 1 is based on the story below**

**After reading the story, enter the details in the map below. This will help you to answer the questions that follow.**

The sky was dark and overcast. It had been raining all night long, and there was no sign of it stopping. I thought that my Sunday would be ruined. As it poured outside, I settled down by the window to watch the rain. The park opposite my house looked even more green and fresh than usual. The branches of the tall trees swayed so hard in the strong wind that I thought they would break. A few children were splashing about in the mud puddles and having a wonderful time. I wished I could join them too! There were very few people out on the road and those who were hurried on their way, wrapped in raincoats and carrying umbrellas.

My mother announced that lunch was ready. It was piping hot and very welcoming in the damp weather. We spent the afternoon listening to music and to the downpour outside.

In the evening, we chatted and made paper boats that we meant to sail in the stream of water outside. It was not a bad day, after all!

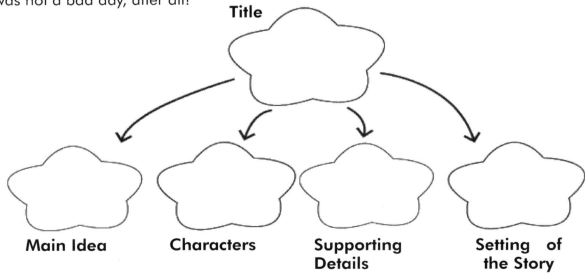

1. What is the setting of the above story?

   Ⓐ  The home of the writer
   Ⓑ  The park
   Ⓒ  The writer's village
   Ⓓ  The writer's office

**Question 2 is based on the story below**

**After reading the story, enter the details in the map below. This will help you to answer the questions that follow.**

One evening, long after most people had gone to bed, a friend and I were making our way merrily back home through the silent and almost deserted streets. We had been to a musical show and were talking about the actor we had seen and heard in it.

"That show made him a star overnight," said my friend about one of the actors. "He was completely unknown before, and now thousands of teenagers send him chocolates and love letters through the mail."

"I thought he was quite good," I said, "but not worth thousands of love letters daily. As a matter of fact, one of his songs gave me pain."

"Which was that?" my friend asked. "Sing to me." I burst into a parody of the song.

"Be quiet for heaven's sake!" My friend gave me an astonished look. "You'll give everybody a fright and wake people up for miles around."

"Never mind," I said, intoxicated with the sound of my own voice. "I don't care. How does it matter?" And I went on singing the latest tunes at the top of my voice. Presently there came behind us the sound of heavy footsteps, and before I could say "Jack Robinson," a policeman was standing in front of me, his notebook open, and a determined look on his face.

"Excuse me, sir," he said. "You have a remarkable voice if I may say so. Who taught you to sing? I'd very much like to find someone who can give my daughter singing lessons. Would you be kind enough to tell me your name and address? Then my wife or I can drop you a line and discuss the matter."

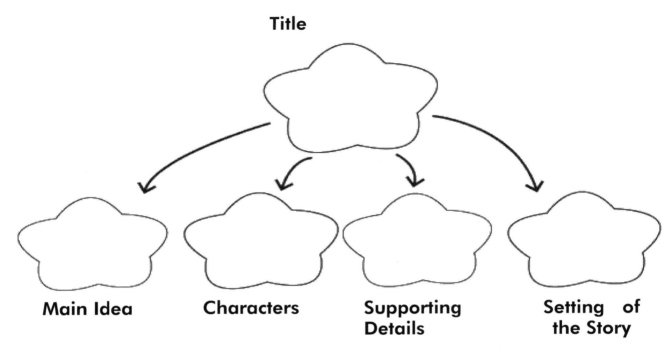

2. **What detail in the above story tells us that it took place late in the night?**

   Ⓐ We had been to a musical show
   Ⓑ "Be quiet for heaven's sake."
   Ⓒ One evening, long after most people had gone to bed
   Ⓓ And I went on singing the latest tunes at the top of my voice

**Question 3 and 4 are based on the story below**

**After reading the story, enter the details in the map below. This will help you to answer the questions that follow.**

Sally woke up earlier than she expected one morning. Something wasn't right. She then realized what had awakened her. It was an unfamiliar sound. She listened closely and realized that the sound was coming from outside. Climbing out of her bed, she slipped into her robe and slippers and went to the window. Looking out, she soon spotted a small kitten under the tree that stood outside her window. She stood, staring at the helpless creature. It didn't move. It soon spotted her and meowed, as if it were calling out to her.

Sally left her room and found her mother in the kitchen having her morning cup of coffee. She excitedly told her mom about the kitten. "I am going outside to get the poor little thing," she told her mother.

"I'll go with you," her mom replied. Together they walked into the backyard. The kitten was still there waiting for them. Sally picked it up in her arms. The little kitten felt so soft and cuddly in her arms. She had always wanted a kitten and wondered if her mother would allow her to keep him. Her mother decided to first feed the kitten. She also decided to make a few calls to see where he came from. The kitten certainly needed a home. Sally became more hopeful that she would be able to keep the kitten.

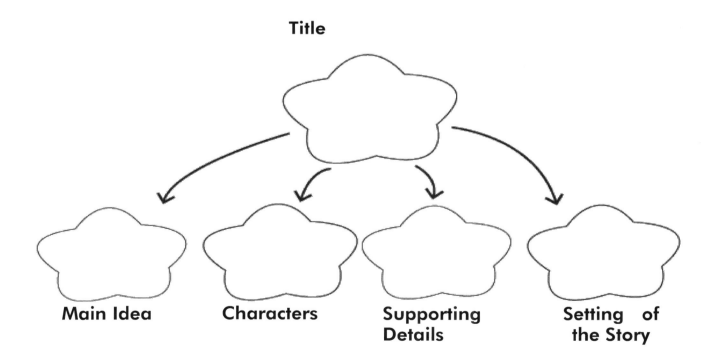

### 3. What sentence(s) point(s) out the time of the story?

- Ⓐ Sally went out of her room and found her mother in the kitchen having her morning cup of coffee
- Ⓑ Sally went out of her room and found her mother in the kitchen.
- Ⓒ Sally woke up earlier than she expected one morning.
- Ⓓ Both A and C

### 4. From the story, we come to know that Sally lived _____.

- Ⓐ in a multi-storied building
- Ⓑ in a downtown, urban area
- Ⓒ in a motel
- Ⓓ in a single family house with a backyard

**Question 5 is based on the poem below**

The forest's sentinel
Glides silently across the hill
And perches in an old pine tree,
A friendly presence his!
No harm can come
From night bird on the prowl.
His cry is mellow,
Much softer than a peacock's call.

Why then this fear of owls
Calling in the night?
If men must speak,
Then owls must hoot-
They have the right.
On me it casts no spell:
Rather, it seems to cry,
"The night is good- all's well, all's well."

-- RUSKIN BOND

### 5. The setting of this poem is in a _____.

- Ⓐ Sports stadium
- Ⓑ Forest
- Ⓒ House
- Ⓓ Palace

**6. What is the setting of a story?**

Ⓐ Who and where the story takes place
Ⓑ When and where the story takes place
Ⓒ When and why the story takes place
Ⓓ How and where the story takes place

**Question 7 is based on the story below**

Ralphie lived in the oldest and largest house on the block. Ralphie's friends were scared to visit him because of how worn down his house looked. The outside of the house was gray with cracks in the stucco and lots of spider webs hanging off it.

**7. What is the setting of the story?**

Ⓐ Inside Ralphie's house
Ⓑ Inside Ralphie's friends' houses
Ⓒ Outside Ralphie's house
Ⓓ None of the above

**Question 8 is based on the story below**

The thieves intended to rob the bank around dinner time. They figured most people would be home eating with their families, so it would be easy for them to get in and out of the big green and gold bank.

**8. What is the setting of the story?**

Ⓐ The bank on Green Street
Ⓑ The bank on Green Street at 7 pm
Ⓒ The green and gold bank at dinner time
Ⓓ The green and gold bank in the morning

### Question 9 is based on the paragraph below

Janice had her last final exam of the year; she was very excited and wanted to celebrate. After this final, she would no longer be a high school student.

**9. In what month was it most likely this last exam occurred?**

- Ⓐ In April
- Ⓑ In June
- Ⓒ In September
- Ⓓ In December

### Question 10 is based on the paragraph below

Noah was excited that he got to share his birthday with his aunt. They were both born on the same day, just nineteen years apart. Their birthday was on April 13th.

**10. In what season is Noah's birthday?**

- Ⓐ In the spring
- Ⓑ In the summer
- Ⓒ In the winter
- Ⓓ In the fall

### Question 11 is based on the paragraph below

Tom looked out his window as he spoke on the phone with his mother. He told her about his day and the new job he just was offered. When Tom talked on the phone, he often looked out the window and would see Thomas Jefferson's monument. It was amazing that he lived in a city with so many beautiful, historical monuments, the White House and the U.S. Capital.

**11. Where does Tom live?**

- Ⓐ New York City
- Ⓑ Washington State
- Ⓒ Delaware
- Ⓓ Washington, D.C.

### Question 12 is based on the poem below

## The Road Not Taken, By Robert Frost

Two roads diverged in a yellow wood,
And sorry I could not travel both
And be one traveler, long I stood
And looked down one as far as I could
To where it bent in the undergrowth;

Then took the other, as just as fair,
And having perhaps the better claim,
Because it was grassy and wanted wear;
Though as for that the passing there
Had worn them really about the same,

And both that morning equally lay
In leaves no step had trodden black.
Oh, I kept the first for another day!
Yet knowing how way leads on to way,
I doubted if I should ever come back.

I shall be telling this with a sigh
Somewhere ages and ages hence:
Two roads diverged in a wood, and
I took the one less traveled by,
And that has made all the difference.

**12. Find the rhyming pattern and describe it. Write your answer in the box below.**

Do NOT write your answers in this book. To open the answer sheet, scan the QR code or visit **lumoslearning.com/a/6e010**

# Chapter 1 → Lesson 10: Author's Purpose in a Text

**Question 1-3 are based on the paragraph below**

**In the original version of the story "The Three Little Pigs," the wolf chases the pigs and says he will huff and puff and blow their houses down.**

**The following paragraph is a different interpretation.**

I've always been misunderstood. I'm allergic to hay. I can't help it that when I'm near hay, I huff and I puff and I sometimes blow things down. No one has any reason to be afraid of me, but sometimes they are. What happened to those poor little pigs is sad, but it was their own fault.

**1. Who is talking in this paragraph? _____**

**2. How is the narrator's point of view different from the traditional one?**

- Ⓐ He claims that he had no intention of blowing down the pigs' houses or of eating them, but that his allergies were at fault.
- Ⓑ He claims that he had no intention of blowing down the pigs' house, but wanted to eat them up.
- Ⓒ He claims that he had no intention of blowing down the pigs' houses or of eating them, but he just wanted to scare them.
- Ⓓ He claims that another wolf blew the pigs' houses down and blamed it on him.

**3. Why does the narrator claim to have been misunderstood?**

- Ⓐ Because everyone has regarded him as a bully who wants to occupy weaker animals' houses
- Ⓑ Because everyone has regarded him as a pig-killing villain when he had no such intention.
- Ⓒ Because everyone has regarded him sick and allergy-ridden.
- Ⓓ Because he is evil.

### Question 4 is based on the sentence below

I was shaking like a leaf. My palms were sweaty and I was so nervous about my presentation.

**4. What point of view is this from?**

Ⓐ Third person omniscient
Ⓑ Second person
Ⓒ First person
Ⓓ Third person

### Question 5 is based on the details below

Heather loved her new dog. She played with it every day and took it for walks. The dog became Heather's best friend, and they did everything together.

**5. What point of view is this told in?**

Ⓐ First person
Ⓑ Second person
Ⓒ Third person
Ⓓ None of the above

### Question 6-8 are based on the passage below

**In the original version of "Little Red Riding Hood," Red is delivering food to her sick grandmother when she stumbles upon a wolf in the house.**

**The following is a different interpretation of "Little Red Riding Hood,"**

I'd been after that wolf for a long time, but when I went into the woods that day to deliver a basket to my grandmother, I promised my mother that I wouldn't leave the path to go wolf-hunting, even if I got a clear shot. I even spoke politely to him and did exactly as my mother asked. But when I got to grandma's house, I found that he had eaten her! I was determined to get revenge. Thank goodness the woodcutter came along and did my job for me. I don't need to get into any trouble with my mother, but it really burns me up when people think I couldn't have handled the wolf by myself!

**6. Who is talking in this passage?**

Ⓐ Red Riding Hood in the story "Little Red Riding Hood"
Ⓑ The wolf in the story "Little Red Riding Hood"
Ⓒ The mother in the story "Little Red Riding Hood"
Ⓓ A narrator

## 7. How is the narrator's point of view different from the traditional one?

Ⓐ She is traditionally thought of as a brave girl who wanted to fight the wily wolf.
Ⓑ The narrator's point of view is not different from the traditional one.
Ⓒ She is traditionally thought of as an innocent child, in danger from the wily wolf.
Ⓓ She is thought of as a mean girl who hates wolfs.

## 8. Why does the narrator claim to have been misunderstood?

Ⓐ She wanted people to think that she is a brave girl.
Ⓑ People think she couldn't have defeated the wolf.
Ⓒ People think that she does not follow her mother's instructions.
Ⓓ Both A and B

**Question 9-11 are based on the poem below**

The forest's sentinel
Glides silently across the hill
And perches in an old pine tree,
A friendly presence his!
No harm can come
From night bird on the prowl.
His cry is mellow,
Much softer than a peacock's call.

Why then this fear of owls
Calling in the night?
If men must speak,
Then owls must hoot-
They have the right.
On me it casts no spell:
Rather, it seems to cry,
"The night is good- all's well, all's well."

-- RUSKIN BOND

## 9. In the above poem the author says 'If men must speak, Then owls must hoot-They have the right.' What does he mean by this?

Ⓐ That people should hoot like owls.
Ⓑ That owls should talk like people.
Ⓒ That owls hoot for the same reasons people speak. This is the way owls communicate.
Ⓓ That owls do not have the right to talk.

**10. Which of the following are usually written in the second person point of view?**

Ⓐ Instructions
Ⓑ Self-help books
Ⓒ Directions
Ⓓ All of the above

**11. What does the poet say in regards to the two roads? Choose all that apply.**

Ⓐ One of the roads is less traveled.
Ⓑ He chose the one less traveled.
Ⓒ He might try the first road another day, but doubts he will return.
Ⓓ He doesn't like the looks of the railroad.

Do NOT write your answers in this book. To open the answer sheet, scan the QR code or visit **lumoslearning.com/a/6e011**

## Chapter 1 → Lesson 11: Compare Author's Writing to Another

### Question 1 is based on the quotations below

"If your actions inspire others to dream more, learn more, do more and become more, you are a leader." - John Quincy Adams

"The key to successful leadership today is influence, not authority." - Kenneth Blanchard

**1. Pick the right statement that brings out the meaning of the above quotations.**

Ⓐ Adams talks about actions, whereas Blanchard talks of authority.
Ⓑ Adams talks about leadership by inspiration, whereas Blanchard talks of leadership by influence.
Ⓒ Adams talks about inspiration, whereas Blanchard talks of influence.
Ⓓ Adams talks about leadership, whereas Blanchard talks of success.

### Question 2 and 3 are based on the passage below

The square is probably the best known of the quadrilaterals shapes. It is defined as having all sides equal. All its interior angles are right angles (90°). From this it follows that the opposite sides are also parallel. A square is simply a specific case of a regular polygon, in this case with 4 sides. All the facts and properties described for regular polygons apply to a square.

The rectangle, like the square, is one of the most commonly known quadrilaterals shapes. It is defined as having all four interior angles 90° (right angles). The opposite sides of a rectangle are parallel and congruent.

**2. A similarity between a square and rectangle is that _____.**

Ⓐ all the sides are equal in both the figures
Ⓑ only opposite sides are equal in both the figures
Ⓒ all the interior angles are right angles
Ⓓ none of the angles are right angles

3. Fill in the Blank

   A difference between a square and rectangle is that _____.

> **Question 4 and 5 are based on the quotations below**

1. Teachers who inspire know that teaching is like cultivating a garden, and those who would have nothing to do with thorns must never attempt to gather flowers.
~Author Unknown

2. Teachers who inspire realize that there will always be rocks in the road ahead of us. They will be stumbling blocks or stepping stones; it all depends on how we use them.
~Author Unknown

4. While the first author says that teaching is like cultivating a garden, the second author says that _____.

   Ⓐ those teachers who would have nothing to do with thorns must never attempt to gather flowers
   Ⓑ inspiring teachers realize that there will be rocks in the road ahead
   Ⓒ inspiring teachers realize that there will only be stepping stones in the road
   Ⓓ inspiring teachers realize that there will be only flowers and no thorns

5. Both the quotations are about _____.

   Ⓐ stumbling blocks
   Ⓑ rocks and stepping stones
   Ⓒ gardens, flowers and thorns
   Ⓓ teachers who inspire

6. Hurricanes are similar to blizzards because _____.

   Ⓐ They both are rain storms.
   Ⓑ They both cause heavy destruction.
   Ⓒ They both are man-made storms.
   Ⓓ They both involve snow.

7. Love is _____ to a roller coaster because there are many twists in turns in both.

   Ⓐ different
   Ⓑ unequal
   Ⓒ similar
   Ⓓ All of the above

### Question 8 is based on the sentence below

When you wash dishes, you want to make sure you use soap to scrub the dirt off and make sure you rinse them clean after.

**8. Which of the tasks below are similar to washing dishes?**

- Ⓐ Cleaning your house
- Ⓑ Washing the laundry
- Ⓒ Folding your clothes
- Ⓓ Cooking dinner

**9. Which of the following terms is used to compare things?**

- Ⓐ Like
- Ⓑ Same as
- Ⓒ Both A and B
- Ⓓ In Contrast

**10. A word that is used to contrast two things is _____.**

- Ⓐ too
- Ⓑ however
- Ⓒ more
- Ⓓ and

# End of Reading Literature

# Chapter 2
# Reading Informational Text

Do NOT write your answers in this book. To open the answer sheet, scan the QR code or visit *lumoslearning.com/a/6e012*

## Lesson 1: Cite Textual Evidence to Support Analysis

**Question 1 and 2 are based on the passage below**

Everywhere around us, there are millions of tiny living things called germs. They are so tiny that they can be seen only under the most powerful microscope. Some of these germs are no wider than twenty-five thousandths of an inch!

Louis Pasteur, the great French scientist, was the first to prove that germs exist. The germs in the air can be counted. The number of germs around us, especially in crowded rooms, is tremendous. Certain scientists counted 42,000 germs in approximately one cubic meter of air in a picture gallery when it was empty. But when the gallery was crowded with people, they found nearly 5,000,000 germs in the same place. In the open-air, germs are less abundant. There are fewer germs in the country air than in town air. We see at once how important it is, therefore, to live as much as possible in the open air, and for the rooms, we live in to always be well ventilated by fresh air.

1. According to the passage, where will you find more germs?

   Ⓐ In crowded spaces
   Ⓑ In the country
   Ⓒ In hospitals
   Ⓓ In empty rooms

2. Which of the following statements can be concluded after reading the passage?

   Ⓐ Louis Pasteur liked counting germs.
   Ⓑ Germs are too small to be seen.
   Ⓒ People have germs.
   Ⓓ Fresher air has fewer germs.

**Question 3-5 are based on the passage below**

George Washington was the first and most popular U.S. President. He was the only one elected by a unanimous vote. It is often said of him that he was "first in war, first in peace, and first in the hearts of his countrymen." Washington led comparatively untrained and ill-equipped American soldiers to victory over the well-trained British in the Revolutionary War. As soon as the Constitution was ratified, he was chosen to be president.

Many of the generals who had fought under Washington did not believe that the 13 colonies could cooperate to form a single country without the strong leadership of a king. They approached him, saying that they would support him as King George I of the United States. Washington was dismayed at the idea, and asked the generals to promise never to mention it again. He served two terms as president and refused a third term, retiring to his farm in Virginia. When England's King George heard that Washington had voluntarily given up the power of the presidency, he said, "If that is true, he is the greatest man in history."

3. How does the author show that George Washington is a great man?

   Ⓐ  He led untrained soldiers into battle.
   Ⓑ  He was unanimously elected president.
   Ⓒ  He voluntarily gave up the power of the presidency.
   Ⓓ  All of the above.

4. Based upon the above story about George Washington, which of the following words best describe him?

   Ⓐ  Smart
   Ⓑ  Power hungry
   Ⓒ  Strong leader
   Ⓓ  Kind

5. According to the text, why was Washington considered the most popular president?

   Ⓐ  King George I said, "He is the greatest man in history."
   Ⓑ  He was elected president by a unanimous vote.
   Ⓒ  He wanted to be a powerful man and king.
   Ⓓ  He was the first president.

### Question 6 is based on the passage below

When Westinghouse, the inventor of the air brake, was working on his great invention, he made an application for a trial of his device to the New York Central Railroad. Vanderbilt, the president of the railroad, thought the inventor's claims were absurd. In comparison with the hand brake then in use, Westinghouse stated that one man instead of two could operate his brake and that his brake would stop a fifty-car train in fifty yards, compared to a sixty-five car train in two hundred yards with hand brakes.

It is said that Vanderbilt roared with laughter. The idea of stopping a train of cars using airpower appeared to be a joke to him. So, he returned the letter, with these words scribbled at the bottom: "I have no time to waste on fools."

The young inventor next turned to the head of another railroad. He was younger and more progressive than his New York rival. He sent for Westinghouse, listened to his explanations, and even advanced him money to continue his experiments. Best of all, he tested the new brake and found that Westinghouse was on the right track. Vanderbilt, hearing of the test, regretted his curt dismissal of the idea. He wrote a courteous note to the inventor, fixing a time for an interview. The note came back with the brief inscription: "I have no time to waste on fools," George Westinghouse.

**6. Which of the following statements can be concluded after reading the passage above?**

Ⓐ Westinghouse was thankful Vanderbilt helped him.
Ⓑ Vanderbilt regretted not listening to Westinghouse's ideas.
Ⓒ Westinghouse was a successful train engineer.
Ⓓ Westinghouse's invention was foolish.

### Question 7 and 8 are based on the passage below

Michael Jordan was the greatest basketball player of all time. When he played for the Chicago Bulls, they had one winning season after another. He scored more than 100 points in 1,108 games, won two Olympic gold medals, and was ranked #1 by ESPN Magazine. Chosen for the NBA All-Stars 14 times, Jordan was ten times the scoring champ, five times the Most Valuable Player, and six times the scoring champ of the NBA. When he began losing his hair, he shaved his head completely and started a fashion trend for other players. He was chosen to make an animated movie called "Space Jam" with Bugs Bunny. No other player has come close to those achievements.

7. According to the passage, which of the following is NOT a reason why Michael Jordan is considered the greatest basketball player of all time?

Ⓐ Michael Jordan shaved his head.
Ⓑ Michael Jordan won two gold medals in the Olympics.
Ⓒ Michael Jordan scored more than 100 points in 1,108 games.
Ⓓ Michael Jordan was the Most Valuable Player five times.

8. Why did the author write this passage about Michael Jordan?

Ⓐ To describe about how Michael Jordan made a movie with Bugs Bunny.
Ⓑ To show what a great basketball player Michael Jordan is.
Ⓒ To give readers Michael Jordan's life story.
Ⓓ To tell people what it is like to be a famous basketball player.

**Question 9 and 10 are based on the passage below**

Most of the planets in our solar system have moons. Saturn has the most, with eighteen moons. Jupiter has sixteen; Uranus has fifteen. Earth has only one, but our moon has a big influence on the lives of humans on Earth. In ancient times, people believed that moonlight could affect people's brains. The Latin word for the moon was Luna. Words like "lunatic" and "looney" come from that idea. Many people still believe that more babies are born and more people die when the moon is full. Scientific studies that have been done to see whether the numbers of births and deaths actually increase when there is a full moon show that there is no increase. The gravitational pull of the moon affects the tides in the ocean, but does not seem to affect the births and deaths of people. Does the full moon cause people to fall in love? That's another question!

9. What, according to the passage, has a "looney" effect on people?

Ⓐ The tides
Ⓑ Saturn
Ⓒ Babies
Ⓓ The moon

10. After reading this passage, what inference can you make?

Ⓐ People believe the moon causes crazy things to happen.
Ⓑ Moonlight from the Earth's moon is less powerful because we only have one moon.
Ⓒ People believe that births, deaths, and love is not influenced by the moon.
Ⓓ Earth's moon is bigger than Jupiter's.

**Question 11 is based on the lines below**

How does the body know to breathe and move?
The central nervous system tells the body what to do.
The nervous system is made up of nerves, the spinal cord and the brain.

11. **From the above lines, we can infer that the nervous system is the _____ of the human body.**

   **Fill in the blank by choosing the correct option from among the 4 options given below.**

   Ⓐ digesting system
   Ⓑ breathing system
   Ⓒ circulatory system
   Ⓓ control system

Do NOT write your answers in this book. To open the answer sheet, scan the QR code or visit **lumoslearning.com/a/6e013**

# Chapter 2 → Lesson 2: Central Idea of Text

**Question 1 and 2 are based on the sentences below**

1. Books were hard to get for the mountain men among the western settlers.
2. Sometimes a mountain man would carry a single battered book with him for years.
3. Some of the men had Bibles, and others had Shakespeare's plays.
4. Shakespeare was a favorite with mountain men, even if they could not read.
5. When they found someone who could read, he was often asked to read one of Shakespeare's plays to a group over a campfire.
6. There were mountain men who could not sign their own names, but could quote passages of Shakespeare by heart.

1. **Part A**
   **Which sentence best shows the central idea of this paragraph?**

   Ⓐ Sentence #1
   Ⓑ Sentence #6
   Ⓒ Sentence #3
   Ⓓ Sentence #5

   **Part B**
   **Which two sentences best support the answer to Part A**

   Ⓐ Sentences #2 and #6
   Ⓑ Sentences #3 and #5
   Ⓒ Sentences #1 and #2
   Ⓓ Sentences #3 and #6

2. **Which sentence does not directly support the central idea?**

   Ⓐ Sentence #2
   Ⓑ Sentence #3
   Ⓒ Sentence #5
   Ⓓ Sentence #6

**Question 3 is based on the passage below**

The rainforest has many layers. Different plants and animals live in each layer. Some layers get more sunlight than others.

**3. Which is the central idea of the passage?**

Ⓐ We should take care of the rainforest.
Ⓑ There are many layers in the rainforest.
Ⓒ Some layers get sunlight.
Ⓓ Rainforests are too wet.

**4. A main idea is _____, and then there are details that support it.**

Ⓐ specific
Ⓑ general
Ⓒ both specific and general
Ⓓ very detailed

**5. The purpose of supporting details is _____.**

Ⓐ to give you a conclusion
Ⓑ to tell you the point of view of the story
Ⓒ to tell the central idea
Ⓓ to give more information to support the central idea

**Question 6-9 are based on the sentences below**

1. Homophones, homographs, and homonyms have different definitions.
2. Homophones are words that sound the same, but are spelled differently and have different meanings.
3. "The golfer drank tea before tee time."
4. Homographs are words that are spelled the same, but are not pronounced the same way.
5. "The artist is planning to record a new record."
6. When two homographs are also homophones, they are called homonyms: word pairs that are spelled the same and pronounced the same way.
7. "He felt fine after he paid the fine."
8. "You can drink juice from a can."
9. You can remember homographs by remembering that "graph" means to write, as in autograph.
10. You can remember homophones by remembering that "phone" means sound, as in telephone.

6. What is the author's probable purpose in including Sentences #9 and #10?

   Ⓐ Sentences #9 and #10 help the reader remember the definition of homograph and homophone.
   Ⓑ Sentences #9 and #10 help the reader see the difference between a homograph and a homophone.
   Ⓒ Sentences #9 and #10 help the reader understand the definition of a homonym.
   Ⓓ Sentences #9 and #10 help the reader understand the difference between a homophone and a homonym.

7. Which sentence is the central idea of the passage?

   Ⓐ Sentence #1
   Ⓑ Sentence #4
   Ⓒ Sentence #6
   Ⓓ Sentence #10

8. Which sentence is a supporting detail for Sentence #2?

   Ⓐ Sentence #3
   Ⓑ Sentence #4
   Ⓒ Sentence #5
   Ⓓ Sentence #10

9. What sentence is supported by detail in Sentence #7?

   Ⓐ Sentence #8
   Ⓑ Sentence #6
   Ⓒ Sentence #7
   Ⓓ Sentence #5

**Question 10 and 11 are based on the passage below**

Everywhere around us there are millions of tiny living things called germs. They are so tiny that they can be seen only under the most powerful microscope. Some of these germs are no wider than twenty-five thousandth's of an inch!

Louis Pasteur, the great French scientist, was the first to prove that germs exist. The germs in the air can be counted. The number of germs around us, especially in crowded rooms, is tremendous. Certain scientists counted 42,000 germs in approximately one cubic meter of air in a picture gallery when it was empty. But when the gallery was crowded with people, they found nearly 5,000,000 germs in the same place. In the open air germs are less abundant. There are fewer germs in country air than in town air. We see at once how important it is, therefore, to live as much as possible in the open air, and for the rooms we live in to always be well ventilated by fresh air.

**10. What is the above passage primarily about?**

   Ⓐ  The French scientist Louis Pasteur
   Ⓑ  The germs
   Ⓒ  The most powerful microscope
   Ⓓ  Living in the country

**11. What do you understand by reading the first paragraph of the above passage?**

   Ⓐ  Everywhere around us there are millions of tiny living things.
   Ⓑ  They can be seen only under a microscope
   Ⓒ  They are called germs
   Ⓓ  All of the above

### Question 12 is based on the passage below

Washing clothes is a difficult task. The skill has to be learned and mastered. It is a tedious and tiresome process, which often discourages a person from going through the exercise. In spite of the availability of modern detergent powders, it remains a difficult task. An expert knows which parts of the dress need special care and attention. The collars of shirts and the seat and pockets of pants are generally dirtier than the other parts. But to wash well, what you require most is patience and the knowledge of the texture and quality of the cloth you are washing so that you can differentiate between clothes which can be put in warm water and which must never be washed in hot water. Woolen, silk and cotton clothes need different types of washing and detergents. One must have proper knowledge of these before washing clothes.

**12. What is the above passage about?**

Do NOT write your answers in this book. To open the answer sheet, scan the QR code or visit **lumoslearning.com/a/6e014**

# Chapter 2 → Lesson 3: Analyze How People, Events, or Ideas are Presented in Text

**Question 1 and 2 are based on the passage below**

**After reading the story, enter the details in the map below. This will help you to answer the questions that follow.**

Everywhere around us, there are millions of tiny living things called germs. They are so tiny that they can be seen only under the most powerful microscope. Some of these germs are no wider than twenty-five thousandths of an inch!

Louis Pasteur, the great French scientist, was the first to prove that germs exist. The germs in the air can be counted. The number of germs around us, especially in crowded rooms, is tremendous. Certain scientists counted 42,000 germs in approximately one cubic meter of air in a picture gallery when it was empty. But when the gallery was crowded with people, they found nearly 5,000,000 germs in the same place. In the open-air germs are less abundant. There are fewer germs in the country air than in town air. We see at once how important it is, therefore, to live as much as possible in the open air, and for the rooms, we live in to always be well ventilated by fresh air.

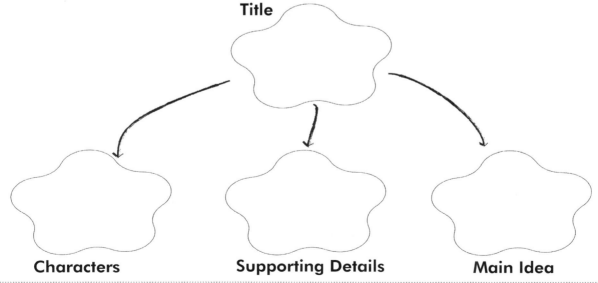

1. What is the central idea of the above passage?

   Ⓐ Louis Pasteur was a great French scientist.
   Ⓑ Germs are everywhere.
   Ⓒ Germs are small.
   Ⓓ Germs can be counted.

2. Which of the following details does NOT support the central idea of the passage?

   Ⓐ Germs are tiny and can only be seen using powerful microscopes.
   Ⓑ There are fewer germs in open air.
   Ⓒ The more people you are around, the sicker you will become.
   Ⓓ Germs are living things.

**Question 3 and 4 are based on the passage below**

**After reading the story, enter the details in the map below. This will help you to answer the questions that follow.**

George Washington was the first and most popular U.S. President. He was the only one elected by a unanimous vote. It is often said of him that he was "first in war, first in peace, and first in the hearts of his countrymen."

Washington led comparatively untrained and ill-equipped American soldiers to victory over the well-trained British in the Revolutionary War. As soon as the Constitution was ratified, he was chosen to be President.

Many of the generals who had fought under Washington did not believe that the 13 colonies could cooperate to form a single country without the strong leadership of a king. They approached him, saying that they would support him as King George I of the United States. Washington was dismayed at the idea, and asked the generals to promise never to mention it again. He served two terms as President and refused a third term, retiring to his farm in Virginia. When England's King George heard that Washington had voluntarily given up the power of the presidency, he said, "If that is true, he is the greatest man in history."

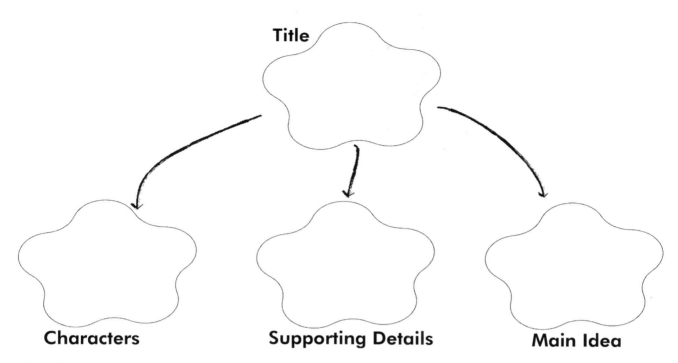

3. What is the central idea of the above passage?

   Ⓐ George Washington refused a third term as president.
   Ⓑ King George said that Washington is a great man.
   Ⓒ George Washington was also known as King George I of the United States.
   Ⓓ George Washington was a general and the first president of United States of America.

4. Based upon the above story about George Washington, which of the following words best describe him?

   Ⓐ Smart
   Ⓑ Power hungry
   Ⓒ Strong leader
   Ⓓ Kind

**Question 5 and 6 are based on the passage below**

When Michael Jordan played for the Chicago Bulls, they had one winning season after another. He scored more than 100 points in 1,108 games, won two Olympic gold medals, and was ranked #1 by ESPN Magazine. Chosen for the NBA All-Stars 14 times, Jordan was ten times the scoring champ, five times the Most Valuable Player, and six times the scoring champ of the NBA. When he began losing his hair, he shaved his head completely and started a fashion trend for other players. He was chosen to make an animated movie called "Space Jam" with Bugs Bunny. No other player has come close to those achievements.

5. **Which of the following would be the best introductory, or topic sentence, for the above passage?**

    Ⓐ  Michael Jordan is often considered to be the greatest basketball player of all time.
    Ⓑ  Michael Jordan loves playing basketball.
    Ⓒ  When Michael Jordan isn't playing basketball he is starring in movies.
    Ⓓ  Michael Jordan won games, medals, and awards as a basketball player.

6. **Which of the following sentences best supports the central idea of the passage?**

    Ⓐ  Michael Jordan was scoring champ of the NBA six times.
    Ⓑ  Michael Jordan scored more than 100 points in 1,108 games.
    Ⓒ  Michael Jordan is best friends with Bugs Bunny.
    Ⓓ  Both A and B.

**Question 7-9 are based on the passage below**

When Westinghouse, the inventor of the air brake, was working on his great invention, he made an application for a trial of his device to the New York Central Railroad. Vanderbilt, the president of the railroad, thought the inventor's claims were absurd. In comparison with the hand brake then in use, Westinghouse stated that one man instead of two could operate his brake and that his brake would stop a fifty-car train in fifty yards, compared to a sixty-five car train in two hundred yards with hand brakes.

It is said that Vanderbilt roared with laughter. The idea of stopping a train of cars by wind appeared to him to be a joke. So he returned the letter, with these words scribbled at the bottom: "I have no time to waste on fools."

The young inventor next turned to the head of another railroad. He was younger and more progressive than his New York rival. He sent for Westinghouse, listened to his explanations, and even advanced him money to continue his experiments. Best of all, he tested the new brake and found that Westinghouse was on the right track. Vanderbilt, hearing of the test, regretted his curt dismissal of the idea. He wrote a courteous note to the inventor, fixing a time for an interview. The note came back with the brief inscription: "I have no time to waste on fools," George Westinghouse.

**7. What is the above passage mostly about?**

- Ⓐ Railroads during the 1800s
- Ⓑ Vanderbilt and his dislike for fools
- Ⓒ Air brakes
- Ⓓ George Westinghouse's invention

**8. How did Westinghouse react to Vanderbilt's dismissal of his idea?**

- Ⓐ Westinghouse gave up.
- Ⓑ Westinghouse kept trying.
- Ⓒ Westinghouse got mad at Vanderbilt.
- Ⓓ Westinghouse decided to try inventing something else.

**9. What kind of person does the passage illustrate George Westinghouse to be?**

- Ⓐ Foolish
- Ⓑ Smart
- Ⓒ Determined
- Ⓓ Courteous

**Question 10 is based on the passage below**

Books were hard to get for the mountain men among the western settlers. Sometimes a mountain man would carry a single battered book with him for years. Some of the men had Bibles, and others had Shakespeare's plays. Shakespeare was a favorite with mountain men, even if they could not read. When they found someone who could read, he was often asked to read one of Shakespeare's plays to a group over a campfire. There were mountain men who could not sign their own names, but could quote passages of Shakespeare by heart.

**10. How does the author of the above passage show that books were important to mountain men?**

- Ⓐ Books were hard for mountain men to get.
- Ⓑ Some mountain men had Shakespeare's plays.
- Ⓒ Some mountain men could quote Shakespeare.
- Ⓓ Not all mountain men could read.

### Question 11 is based on the passage below

Washing clothes is a difficult task. The skill has to be learned and mastered. It is a tedious and tiresome process, which often discourages a person from going through the exercise. In spite of the availability of modern detergent powders, it remains a difficult task. An expert knows which parts of the clothing needs special care and attention. The collars of shirts and the seat and pockets of pants are generally dirtier than the other parts. But to wash well, what you require most is patience and the knowledge of the texture and quality of the cloth you are washing so that you can differentiate between clothes which can be put in warm water and clothes which must never be washed in hot water. Woolens, silk and cotton clothes need different types of washing and detergents. One must have proper knowledge of this before washing clothes.

**11. How does the author of the above passage illustrate that washing clothes is a difficult task?**

Ⓐ By discussing the different types of washing machines.
Ⓑ By pointing out that certain parts of clothing need special care and attention.
Ⓒ By talking about all the different laundry detergent options.
Ⓓ By explaining how time consuming laundry can be.

Do NOT write your answers in this book. To open the answer sheet, scan the QR code or visit **lumoslearning.com/a/6e015**

# Chapter 2 → Lesson 4: Determine Technical Meanings

1. What is a synonym of a word?

    Ⓐ A word that has the same meaning as the given word.
    Ⓑ A word that has the opposite meaning of a given word.
    Ⓒ A word that has the same spelling as the given word.
    Ⓓ A word that has the same pronunciation as the given word.

2. Which of the following statements is true about antonyms?

    Ⓐ They have the same meaning as the given word.
    Ⓑ They are the definitions of a given word.
    Ⓒ They have the same sounds as a given word.
    Ⓓ They are the opposites of a given word.

**Question 3 is based on the sentence below**

The words "minute" (time) and "minute" (extremely small) are pronounced differently and have different meanings.

3. These types of words are called _____.

    Ⓐ Homophones
    Ⓑ Homonyms
    Ⓒ Homographs
    Ⓓ Homo-words

4. Which of the choices below is an example of an "antonym"?

    Ⓐ Clever, crazy
    Ⓑ Pretty, beautiful
    Ⓒ Narrow, skinny
    Ⓓ Abundant, scarce

5. Which of the choices below is an example of synonyms?

   Ⓐ  mini, tiny
   Ⓑ  clever, foolish
   Ⓒ  good, bad
   Ⓓ  soggy, dry

6. Choose the correct set of antonyms from the following.

   Ⓐ  courteous, kind
   Ⓑ  regretted, refused
   Ⓒ  brief, small
   Ⓓ  stopped, started

7. Choose the set of rhyming words from the following.

   Ⓐ  fresh, air
   Ⓑ  space, spread
   Ⓒ  worms, germs
   Ⓓ  breathe, breath

8. A group of words that share the same spelling and pronunciation but have different meanings is called a _____.

   Ⓐ  Synonym
   Ⓑ  Homonym
   Ⓒ  Syllable
   Ⓓ  Consonant

9. Which of the following statements defines homophones?

   Ⓐ  The words that have the same meaning and different spellings.
   Ⓑ  The words that have the same sound but different meanings.
   Ⓒ  The words that have the same sound but have different meanings and spellings.
   Ⓓ  The words that do not have the same sound but have the same meaning and spelling.

10. Identify the correct set of homophones from the following.

    Ⓐ  mustard, mustered
    Ⓑ  loan, lone
    Ⓒ  lumbar, lumber
    Ⓓ  both A and B

11. **Part A**

A word that has the same meaning or nearly the same meaning as another word is a (an) _____.

Ⓐ Antonym
Ⓑ Synonym
Ⓒ Homophone
Ⓓ Rhyme

**Part B**

A word that has the opposite meaning to another is a (an) _____.

Ⓐ Antonym
Ⓑ Synonym
Ⓒ Homophone
Ⓓ Rhyme

Do NOT write your answers in this book. To open the answer sheet, scan the QR code or visit **lumoslearning.com/a/6e016**

# Chapter 2 → Lesson 5: Structure of Text

1. **Identify where the underlined sentence below belongs in the paragraph.**

<u>Start with the freshest bread you can find.</u>

I will tell you how to make a perfect peanut butter sandwich.
Take the two pieces of bread.
Add a good-sized scoop of crunchy peanut butter, and be sure to spread it on both pieces of bread.
Find a jar of your favorite jam.
Use slightly less jam than peanut butter, and spread it on only one slice of bread.
Put the two slices together and cut the sandwich in half. Enjoy.

Ⓐ The missing sentence should be first.
Ⓑ The missing sentence should be second.
Ⓒ The missing sentence should be third.
Ⓓ The missing sentence should be fourth.

2. **Identify where the underlined sentence below belongs in the paragraph.**

<u>During the pre-competition phase, continue the aerobic training, but add strength training and sprints</u>.

Training for tennis can be broken down into four phases.
During the preparation phase, work on aerobic fitness with jogging, swimming, or cycling as you train heavily on the specifics of tennis.
While competing, training can ease up except for the specifics of tennis.
For several weeks after competition, rest from playing tennis but keep up your fitness by playing other sports.

Ⓐ The missing sentence should be first.
Ⓑ The missing sentence should be second.
Ⓒ The missing sentence should be third.
Ⓓ The missing sentence should be fourth.

**3. Identify where the underlined sentence below belongs in the paragraph.**

<u>**In French, the word means "rotten pot."**</u>

Today we have spray cans for freshening the air, but it's more fun to make a potpourri. Potpourris were originally made in France by creating a mixture of flower petals and leaves that was allowed to sit in a crock for months. Today, many people still like to make potpourris from herbs and flowers. You can make your own from herbs and flowers from the garden.

- Ⓐ The missing sentence should be first.
- Ⓑ The missing sentence should be second.
- Ⓒ The missing sentence should be third.
- Ⓓ The missing sentence should be fourth.

**4. Arrange the sentences below in the most logical order.**

1. On the front of each cap is a white horse.
2. The caps also have the motto, "They fear no difficulty."
3. Officers can be identified by the crimson sash worn over their shoulders.
4. The tallest men have high bearskin caps.
5. The British troops present a colorful appearance.
6. Crowds gather to watch the elegant soldiers parade by.

- Ⓐ 6, 1, 2, 5, 4, 3
- Ⓑ 5, 3, 4, 1, 2, 6
- Ⓒ 5, 4, 3, 6, 1, 2
- Ⓓ 1, 2, 3, 4, 5, 6

**5. Arrange the sentences in the most logical order.**

1. Most farm families raised geese, so goose feathers were plentiful.
2. Colonists also used the feathers of wild turkeys and hawks.
3. Crow feathers were harder to collect, but were considered the best for making fine lines.
4. Colonists often made their quill pens from goose feathers.

- Ⓐ 4, 1, 2, 3
- Ⓑ 1, 2, 3, 4
- Ⓒ 3, 2, 1, 4
- Ⓓ 2, 3, 1, 4

**6. Arrange the sentences in the most logical order.**

1. Later, European traders spread pineapple growing to Africa and the Pacific Islands, including Hawaii.
2. The name was later changed to pineapple.
3. The name may come from the Dutch word for pinecone, which is pi jnappel.
4. Christopher Columbus was the first European to taste what he called "Indian pinecones."

- Ⓐ  4, 3, 2, 1
- Ⓑ  4, 1, 3, 2
- Ⓒ  1, 2, 3, 4
- Ⓓ  3, 2, 1, 4

**Question 7 and 8 are based on the passage below**

When Westinghouse, the inventor of the air brake, was working on his great invention, he made an application for a trial of his device to the New York Central Railroad. Vanderbilt, the president of the railroad, thought the inventor's claims were absurd. In comparison with the hand brake then in use, Westinghouse stated that one man instead of two could operate his brake and that his brake would stop a fifty-car train in fifty yards, compared to a sixty-five car train in two hundred yards with hand brakes.

It is said that Vanderbilt roared with laughter. The idea of stopping a train of cars by wind appeared to him to be a joke. So he returned the letter, with these words scribbled at the bottom: "I have no time to waste on fools."

The young inventor next turned to the head of another railroad. He was younger and more progressive than his New York rival. He sent for Westinghouse, listened to his explanations, and even advanced him money to continue his experiments. Best of all, he tested the new brake and found that Westinghouse was on the right track. Vanderbilt, hearing of the test, regretted his curt dismissal of the idea. He wrote a courteous note to the inventor, fixing a time for an interview. The note came back with the brief inscription: "I have no time to waste on fools," George Westinghouse.

**7. What kind of a writing piece is the above passage?**

- Ⓐ  A personal narrative
- Ⓑ  A persuasive essay
- Ⓒ  An informative/expository passage
- Ⓓ  A journal entry

**8. Which of the following would turn the passage into a personal narrative?**

Ⓐ If the above passage was written by Westinghouse himself.
Ⓑ If the author was President Vanderbilt and he wrote about George Westinghouse.
Ⓒ If the author was a third person.
Ⓓ None of the above

**9. What are the main parts of an essay?**

Ⓐ A topic title
Ⓑ An introduction to the topic
Ⓒ Details about the topic and a conclusion to the topic
Ⓓ All of the above

**10. What are the parts of a business letter?**

Ⓐ The heading, the inside address
Ⓑ The greeting, the body
Ⓒ The complimentary close, the signature line
Ⓓ All of the above

**11. The salutation in a business letter is what part of a letter?**

Ⓐ Heading
Ⓑ Closing
Ⓒ Address and date
Ⓓ Greeting

**12. Which of the following types of writing will most likely contain the most descriptive writing (imagery)?**

Ⓐ Letter of complaint to a store about a product that was faulty
Ⓑ Personal narrative about a rodeo
Ⓒ Descriptive paper about a winter day
Ⓓ Informative/Expository paper about snow

Do NOT write your answers in this book. To open the answer sheet, scan the QR code or visit **lumoslearning.com/a/6e017**

## Chapter 2 → Lesson 6: Determine Author's Point of View

**Question 1 is based on the passage below**

Dogs are better pets than cats for many reasons. Dogs are a man's best friend and can learn tricks. Dogs will get you things when you ask them to. Dogs will go walking or running with you to help keep you in shape. Dogs like to cuddle and protect their owners.

**1. What is the purpose of the above passage?**

Ⓐ  To inform
Ⓑ  To explain
Ⓒ  To persuade
Ⓓ  To entertain

**Question 2 is based on the passage below**

If you invent a new word and enough people like it, you may find it in the dictionary. Dictionaries add new words as they come into common use. The fancy word for a brand-new word is "neologism." In 2011, the Merriam-Webster Collegiate Dictionary added some neologisms you probably know, such as "tweet," "fist bump," and "social media."

Some of the new words may not be so familiar.

- "Planking" is a game of lying face down, hands at your sides, in the most unusual place you can think of, and having your picture taken and posted on the internet.
- A "bromance" is a close friendship – but not a romance – between two men.
- A "robocall" is a call made automatically by a machine repeating a taped message.
- A "helicopter parent" is one who hovers over their children, becoming much too involved in their lives.
- And "crowdsourcing"? That's the way many people can each do a little bit of a very large project.

The country of Iceland, for example, is crowdsourcing a new constitution for their country, so if you have an idea about what they ought to include, you can go online and send them your suggestion.

At the same time new words are being added, old words that are no longer widely recognized are dropped from the dictionary. This year, the dictionary deleted the words "growlery" (a room where you can go to complain) and "brabble" (another word for squabble). If you haven't heard those words before, you probably won't miss them!

**2. What is the purpose of the passage above?**

Ⓐ To inform
Ⓑ To explain
Ⓒ To persuade
Ⓓ To entertain

**Question 3 is based on the passage below**

I will tell you how to make a perfect peanut butter sandwich. Start with the freshest bread you can find. Take two pieces of bread. Add a good-sized scoop of crunchy peanut butter, and be sure to spread it on both pieces of bread. Find a jar of your favorite jam. Use slightly less jam than peanut butter, and spread it on only one slice of bread. Put the two slices together and cut the sandwich in half. Enjoy.

**3. Part A**
**What is the purpose of the passage above?**

Ⓐ To inform
Ⓑ To explain
Ⓒ To persuade
Ⓓ To entertain

**Part B**
**What point of view is the paragraph above told from?**

Ⓐ First person
Ⓑ Second person
Ⓒ Third person
Ⓓ Fourth person

**Question 4 is based on the passage below**

Everywhere around us, there are millions of tiny living things called germs. They are so tiny that they can be seen only under the most powerful microscope. Some of these germs are no wider than twenty-five thousandths of an inch!

Louis Pasteur, the great French scientist, was the first to prove that germs exist. The germs in the air can be counted. The number of germs around us, especially in crowded rooms, is tremendous. Certain scientists counted 42,000 germs in approximately one cubic meter of air in a picture gallery when it was empty. But when the gallery was crowded with people, they found nearly 5,000,000 germs in the same place. In the open-air, germs are less abundant. There are fewer germs in the country air than in town air. We see at once how important it is, therefore, to live as much as possible in the open air, and for the rooms, we live in to always be well ventilated by fresh air.

4. What is the purpose of the passage above?

- Ⓐ To inform
- Ⓑ To explain
- Ⓒ To persuade
- Ⓓ To entertain

**Question 5 is based on the passage below**

Football is the most exciting sport. During a football game, two teams of eleven players battle to reach the end zone. During the game, the players try to catch or run with the ball without being tackled by the opposing team. Sometimes players jump over each other, break tackles, and run as fast as lightning. Football fans cheer extremely loud when their team reaches the end zone. There is never a dull moment in football.

5. What is the purpose of the passage above?

- Ⓐ To convince readers to go to a football game.
- Ⓑ To tell a story about what happened at a football game.
- Ⓒ To explain to readers about what happens at a football game.
- Ⓓ To help the reader understand why to never attend a football game.

**Question 6 is based on the passage below**

Eating carrots, broccoli, and string beans are good for you. Making sure to have healthy vegetables in your diet is important. Some people think eating vegetables at one meal is good enough, but it isn't; you should eat vegetables at least 3 meals a day.

6. What is the purpose of the above passage?

Ⓐ To convince the reader to eat more vegetables.
Ⓑ To give information about different types of vegetables.
Ⓒ To tell about a cartoon where the characters are played by vegetables.
Ⓓ To help the reader understand that vegetables are unimportant.

**Question 7 is based on the passage below**

George Washington was the first and most popular U.S. President. He was the only one elected by a unanimous vote. It is often said of him that he was "first in war, first in peace, and first in the hearts of his countrymen." Washington led comparatively untrained and ill-equipped American soldiers to victory over the well-trained British in the Revolutionary War. As soon as the Constitution was ratified, he was chosen to be President.

Many of the generals who had fought under Washington did not believe that the 13 colonies could cooperate to form a single country without the strong leadership of a king. They approached him, saying that they would support him as King George I of the United States. Washington was dismayed at the idea and asked the generals to promise never to mention it again. He served two terms as President and refused a third term, retiring to his farm in Virginia. When England's King George heard that Washington had voluntarily given up the power of the presidency, he said, "If that is true, he is the greatest man in history."

7. How does the author show that George Washington is a great man?

Ⓐ He led untrained soldiers into battle.
Ⓑ He was unanimously elected president.
Ⓒ He voluntarily gave up the power of the presidency.
Ⓓ All of the above.

### Question 8 is based on the passage below

Michael Jordan was the greatest basketball player of all time. When he played for the Chicago Bulls, they had one winning season after another. He scored more than 100 points in 1,108 games, won two Olympic gold medals, and was ranked #1 by ESPN Magazine. Chosen for the NBA All-Stars 14 times, Jordan was ten times the scoring champ, five times the Most Valuable Player, and six times the scoring champ of the NBA. When he began losing his hair, he shaved his head completely and started a fashion trend for other players. He was chosen to make an animated movie called "Space Jam" with Bugs Bunny. No other player has come close to those achievements.

**8. Why did the author write this passage about Michael Jordan?**

Ⓐ To tell about how Michael Jordan made a movie with Bugs Bunny.
Ⓑ To show what a great basketball player Michael Jordan is.
Ⓒ To give readers Michael Jordan's life story.
Ⓓ To tell people what it is like to be a famous basketball player.

### Question 9 is based on the story below

Most of the planets in our solar system have moons. Saturn has the most, with eighteen moons. Jupiter has sixteen; Uranus has fifteen. Earth has only one, but our moon has a big influence on the lives of humans on earth. In ancient times, people believed that moonlight could affect people's brains. The Latin word for the moon was Luna. Words like "lunatic" and "looney" come from that idea. Many people still believe that more babies are born and more people die when the moon is full. Scientific studies that have been done to see whether the numbers of births and deaths actually increase when there is a full moon show that there is no increase. The gravitational pull of the moon affects the tides in the ocean, but does not seem to affect the births and deaths of people. Does the full moon cause people to fall in love? That's another question!

**9. What point of view is the story above told from?**

Ⓐ First person
Ⓑ Second person
Ⓒ Third person
Ⓓ Fourth person

## Chapter 2 → Lesson 7: Evaluating Arguments in Text

**Question 1 is based on the passage below**

Michael Jordan was the greatest basketball player of all time. He scored more than 100 points in 1,108 games, won two Olympic gold medals, and was ranked #1 by ESPN Magazine. Chosen for the NBA All-Stars 14 times, Jordan was ten times the scoring champ, five times the Most Valuable Player, and six times the scoring champ of the NBA. No other player has come close to those achievements.

1. **Identify the main idea in the above persuasive paragraph.**

   Ⓐ Jordan was six times the 'scoring champ' for NBA.
   Ⓑ Jordan was chosen for the NBA All-Stars 14 times.
   Ⓒ Jordan was the greatest basketball player.
   Ⓓ Jordan was a basketball player.

**Question 2 is based on the passage below**

Michael Jordan was the greatest basketball player of all time. When he played for the Chicago Bulls, they had one winning season after another. When he began losing his hair, he shaved his head completely and started a fashion trend for other players. He was chosen to make an animated movie called "Space Jam" with Bugs Bunny. There are many good players, but Michael Jordan will always be my favorite.

2. **The claim: Jordan was the greatest basketball player.**
   **Which of the following supports this claim?**

   Ⓐ He was the best player on the team.
   Ⓑ When he began losing his hair, he shaved his head completely and started a fashion trend for other players.
   Ⓒ He was chosen to make an animated movie called "Space Jam" with Bugs Bunny.
   Ⓓ When he played for the Chicago Bulls, they had one winning season after another.

**Question 3 and 4 are based on the passage below**

Life in the city is always exciting. There are more than a million people in the city where I live. There are street fairs and sidewalk vendors downtown. Most days, people are going about their daily business, just working. In that way, a big city is no different from a small town. But, in the city, there are many more concerts, lectures, theatrical performances, and other kinds of entertainment. Most of those things are expensive, and I can't afford to go. Because of the curfew, young people aren't allowed on the streets at night, and I usually have a lot of homework.

3. According to the passage, why does the author prefer to live in the city?
   Which of the following are the arguments from the passage that support the above sentence?

   Ⓐ  1. City life is always exciting.
       2. There are one million people living in the city.
   Ⓑ  1. There are street fairs and sidewalk vendors.
       2. There are concerts and all kinds of entertainment.
   Ⓒ  1. Young people aren't allowed on the streets at night.
       2. I have a lot of homework.
   Ⓓ  1. Most of the things are expensive.
       2. I can't afford to go to these exciting places.

4. Why can't young people enjoy city life?
   Which of the following answers this question?

   Ⓐ  1. City life is always exciting.
       2. Too many people live in the city.
   Ⓑ  1. There are street fairs and sidewalk vendors.
       2. There are concerts and all kinds of entertainment.
   Ⓒ  1. There's a curfew for young people at night.
       2. Young people have no time due to too much homework.
   Ⓓ  1. People go about their daily work.
       2. A big city is actually no different from a small town.

**Question 5 is based on the passage below**

Fast food is unhealthy; it leads to obesity and disease, but the convenience and addictiveness of it contribute to the laziness of the general population. Most people eat fast food because they lack time to prepare a more nutritious meal. It seems as though there is a fast food restaurant on every street corner. The general population overlooks the fact that eating nothing but these greasy foods will contribute to weight gain. Fast food is addictive because it is easily accessible and tastes so good.

**5. In the above passage, which sentence supports the argument that fast food contributes to unhealthy weight gain?**

Ⓐ Most people eat fast food because they lack time to prepare a more nutritious meal.
Ⓑ It seems as though there is a fast-food restaurant on every street corner.
Ⓒ The general population overlooks the fact that eating nothing but these greasy foods will cause you to gain weight.
Ⓓ Fast food is addictive for the convenience of it.

### Question 6 is based on the passage below

Kickboxing is a great form of exercise. This type of exercise tones your entire body. Punching a bag helps you gain strength and muscle in your arms. You also use the bag to do different types of kicks, thus strengthening your legs as well. Kickboxing is a total body workout that everyone should try.

**6. The claim: Kickboxing is a great form of exercise.**
**Select the answer that most completely supports the claim:_____**

Ⓐ This exercise routine allows you to use a punching bag.
Ⓑ This exercise strengthens your muscles.
Ⓒ This type of exercise tones your entire body.
Ⓓ Kickboxing is the new trend in exercise routines.

### Question 7 is based on the passage below

Electric cars are a new, innovative type of car that help the environment. They use little to no gas, there by keeping pollutants out of the air. They may be a little more expensive than the average car, but you will make that money back in savings on gas. The electric car is now being made by almost all car companies.

**7. The claim: Electric cars are a new, innovative type of car.**
**Select the option that supports the claim.**

Ⓐ Electric cars are a great way to help the environment.
Ⓑ Electric cars are only a few years old.
Ⓒ Electric cars are expensive.
Ⓓ Most companies are now making electric cars.

### Question 8 is based on the passage below

Running a marathon is a great accomplishment. Training for a marathon takes months. First, you have to start running short distances, and increase the distance you run each week. During your training, you will eventually start running 20 miles at a time. A full marathon is 26.2 miles and very hard for people to finish. With a little time, training and hard work, anyone can run a marathon. Completing the marathon is a great accomplishment because it shows excellent dedication and athletic ability.

**8. What is the central idea or claim of this passage?**

Ⓐ Running a marathon requires you to train a lot.
Ⓑ Running a marathon is a great accomplishment.
Ⓒ Running requires excellent dedication.
Ⓓ Not many people are able to complete a marathon.

### Question 9 is based on the passage below

Smartphones are the newest innovative technology out there. On the smartphone you can video chat with your friends or family members to keep in touch. Smartphones also are a great way to stay organized and keep your life on track. Smartphones are an easy way to search the internet when you are out and need to find something quickly. They allow you to access tons of information.

**9. Which sentence is the claim of the passage?**

### Question 10 is based on the paragraph below

Horses are used for many different types of activities. Horses can be used to pull carts. They are also used for riding English style in which the rider can jump and show them. Horses can also be used for riding Western style in which riders can herd and rope cattle and go on trail rides. An English style rider can also perform dressage, which is a highly precise series of movements involving the rider and the horse.

**10. Identify the claim in this paragraph.**

Ⓐ Dressage is the most intricate form of horse training.
Ⓑ Horses can be used for many different activities.
Ⓒ Horses can be ridden English style.
Ⓓ Horses can be ridden Western style.

**Question 11 is based on the paragraph below**

Michael Phelps is the most decorated American athlete in Olympic history. Michael Phelps has won more gold medals in his swimming career than any other American Olympian. He also has won the most gold medals in one Olympic game. Michael Phelps will become the most decorated Olympian world wide if he wins during the London 2012 summer Olympics.

**11. Identify the claim in this paragraph.**

Do NOT write your answers in this book. To open the answer sheet, scan the QR code or visit *lumoslearning.com/a/6e019*

## Chapter 2 → Lesson 8: Compare/Contrast One Author's Presentation with Another

**Question 1 is based on the quotations below**

"Peace cannot be achieved through violence, it can only be attained through understanding." - Ralph Waldo Emerson

"Peace cannot be kept by force; it can only be achieved by understanding." - Albert Einstein

**1. What views on peace do Einstein and Emerson share?**

Ⓐ You can only have peace by fighting.
Ⓑ You can only have peace through understanding.
Ⓒ You can only have peace when everyone gets along.
Ⓓ Peace is all around us.

**Question 2 is based on the quotations below**

"Music is a world within itself, with a language we all understand." - Stevie Wonder
"Without music, life would be a mistake." - Fredrich Nietzsche

**2. Which of the following statements is true about both Stevie Wonder's and Fredrich Nietzsche's views on music?**

Ⓐ They both believe that music is essential for a meaningful life.
Ⓑ They both believe that music is a universal language.
Ⓒ They both believe that music can be understood by everyone.
Ⓓ They both believe that music has the power to communicate emotions.

**Question 3 is based on the quotations below**

"In every walk with nature one receives far more than he seeks." - John Muir
"Nature always wears the colors of the spirit." - Ralph Waldo Emerson

**3. How do the two authors' presentations of nature differ?**

Ⓐ  Muir believes nature should be explored while Emerson thinks it should be admired from a distance.
Ⓑ  Muir and Emerson both believe nature provides spiritual benefits but Emerson thinks it reflects our internal states while Muir thinks we receive more than we seek.
Ⓒ  Muir and Emerson both believe nature should be used for human benefit.
Ⓓ  Muir and Emerson both believe that humans can control and manipulate nature.

**Question 4 is based on the quotations below**

"Nature does not hurry, yet everything is accomplished." - Lao Tzu
"In every walk with nature, one receives far more than he seeks." - John Muir

**4. Which statement best compares and contrasts the authors' presentations of ideas about nature?**

Ⓐ  Both authors believe that nature is powerful and should be respected, but Lao Tzu emphasizes the importance of patience, while John Muir emphasizes how nature gives more than what you seek
Ⓑ  Both authors believe that nature is a source of inspiration and fulfillment, but Lao Tzu emphasizes the need to take action, while John Muir emphasizes the value of reflection.
Ⓒ  Both authors believe that nature is a teacher and provides valuable lessons, but Lao Tzu emphasizes the need to embrace simplicity, while John Muir emphasizes the need to explore and discover.
Ⓓ  Both authors believe that nature is a harmonious and balanced system, but Lao Tzu emphasizes the need to adapt to its rhythms, while John Muir emphasizes the need to appreciate its diversity.

### Question 5 is based on the quotations below

"The only way to do great work is to love what you do." - Steve Jobs
"Success is not final, failure is not fatal: It is the courage to continue that counts." - Winston Churchill

**5. Which statement accurately contrasts the views of Steve Jobs and Winston Churchill on success?**

Ⓐ  Steve Jobs believed that success comes from loving what you do, while Winston Churchill believed that success is about having the courage to continue.
Ⓑ  Steve Jobs believed that success is not final, failure is not fatal, while Winston Churchill believed that success comes from loving what you do.
Ⓒ  Steve Jobs and Winston Churchill both believed that success comes from having the courage to continue.
Ⓓ  Steve Jobs and Winston Churchill both believed that success comes from loving what you do.

### Question 6 is based on the quotations below

The greatest glory in living lies not in never falling, but in rising every time we fall." - Nelson Mandela
"Success is not the key to happiness. Happiness is the key to success." - Albert Schweitzer

**6. Which statement accurately compares the views of Nelson Mandela and Albert Schweitzer on success?**

Ⓐ  Nelson Mandela and Albert Schweitzer both believe that success lies in overcoming failure.
Ⓑ  Nelson Mandela believes that success lies in overcoming failure, while Albert Schweitzer believes that happiness is the key to success.
Ⓒ  Albert Schweitzer believes that success lies in overcoming failure, while Nelson Mandela believes that happiness is the key to success.
Ⓓ  Nelson Mandela and Albert Schweitzer both believe that happiness is the key to success.

**Question 7 based on the quotations below**

1. "For every disciplined effort there is a multiple reward." - Jim Rohn

2. "Genius is one percent inspiration and ninety-nine percent perspiration." - Thomas Alva Edison

7. Both Edison and Rohn are talking about the benefit of _____.

   Ⓐ genius
   Ⓑ reward
   Ⓒ effort
   Ⓓ inspiration

**Question 8 is based on the quotations below**

"Friendship is not something you learn in school. But if you haven't learned the meaning of friendship, you really haven't learned anything." - Muhammad Ali

"If you live to be 100, I hope to live to be 100 minus 1 day, so I never have to live without you." - Winnie the Pooh

8. What do both of these quotations have in common?

   Ⓐ They are both about living life.
   Ⓑ They are both about friendship.
   Ⓒ They are both about learning.
   Ⓓ They have nothing in common

**Read the quotations and then answer the question that follows.**

"Education is the most powerful weapon which you can use to change the world." Nelson Mandela
"Be the change you wish to see in the world." Gandhi

9. Both of these quotations talk about changing the world. What are the two ways to make change in the world, as per Mandela and Gandhi?

   Ⓐ Education and yourself
   Ⓑ Weapons and yourself
   Ⓒ Yourself and man
   Ⓓ Education and weapons

**Read the quotations and then answer the question that follows.**

"Happiness is not something ready-made. It comes from your own actions." - Dalai Lama
"Success is not in what you have, but who you are." - Bo Bennett

**10. Which statement accurately compares the views of the Dalai Lama and Bo Bennett on happiness and success?**

Ⓐ  The Dalai Lama believes that happiness comes from one's actions, while Bo Bennett believes that success is defined by who you are.
Ⓑ  The Dalai Lama believes that success is not in what you have, while Bo Bennett believes that happiness is defined by your actions.
Ⓒ  The Dalai Lama believes that success is defined by who you are, while Bo Bennett believes that happiness comes from your actions.
Ⓓ  The Dalai Lama believes that success is defined by who you are, while Bo Bennett believes that happiness comes from your actions.

**Read the quotations and then answer the question that follows.**

"If your actions inspire others to dream more, learn more, do more and become more, you are a leader". - John Quincy Adams

"The key to successful leadership today is influence, not authority." - Kenneth Blanchard

**11. The above statements tell us that they are talking about _____.**

# End of Reading Informational Text

# Chapter 3
# Language

Do NOT write your answers in this book. To open the answer sheet, scan the QR code or visit **lumoslearning.com/a/6e020**

# Lesson 1: Correct subject-verb agreement

**1. Correct the following sentence to show subject-verb agreement.**

Tracy and Gary likes to solve puzzles.

Ⓐ Tracy and Gary likes to solve puzzles.
Ⓑ Tracy and Gary like to solve puzzles.
Ⓒ Tracy and Gary like to solves puzzle.
Ⓓ Tracy likes to solve puzzle.

**2. Correct the following sentence to show subject-verb agreement.**

All of the students competes for the prizes.

Ⓐ All of the student competes for the prizes.
Ⓑ All of the students compete for the prizes.
Ⓒ The students competes for the prizes.
Ⓓ None of the above

**3. Correct the following sentence to show subject-verb agreement.**

Many people considers tea a stimulant.

Ⓐ Many a people considers tea a stimulant.
Ⓑ Many people consider tea a stimulant.
Ⓒ Many peoples consider tea a stimulant.
Ⓓ The above sentence needs no correction.

**4. Correct the verb to show correct subject-verb agreement.**

The enemies plots revenge and won the battle this time.

Ⓐ The enemy plot revenge and win the battle this time.
Ⓑ The enemy plot revenge and will win the battle this time.
Ⓒ The enemy will plot revenge and will won the battle this time.
Ⓓ The enemies plot revenge and win the battle this time.

**5. Which of the following sentences corrects the given sentence by using the tenses correctly?**

Sally finish her project earlier than the others.

Ⓐ Sally finish her projects earlier than the others.
Ⓑ Sally finished her project earlier than the others.
Ⓒ Sally have already finish her project earlier than the others.
Ⓓ Sally finishing her project earlier than the others.

**6. Which of the following options correctly fills in the blank in the following sentence?**

Some of the votes _____ to have been miscounted.

Ⓐ seems
Ⓑ seem
Ⓒ will seem
Ⓓ shall seem

**7. Which of the following options correctly fills in the blank in the following sentence?**

All of the dancers_____ to be sick.

Ⓐ appear
Ⓑ has appeared
Ⓒ will appear
Ⓓ appears

**8. Which of the following options correctly fills in the blank in the following sentence?**

Parents and students _____ against the hike in tuition fee.

Ⓐ is
Ⓑ are
Ⓒ are being
Ⓓ had been

**9. Which of the following options correctly fills in the blank in the following sentence?**

Either the Principal in this School or the Chief Administrator _____ to make a quick decision.

Ⓐ have
Ⓑ will
Ⓒ has
Ⓓ are

**10. Which of the following options correctly fills in the blank in the following sentence?**

She seems to forget that there _____ things to be done before the expedition.

Ⓐ is
Ⓑ has
Ⓒ are
Ⓓ have

**11. Correct the following sentence to show subject-verb agreement.**

The girls' shirt is lime green.

**12. Correct the following sentence to show subject-verb agreement.**

Tony climb the tree every day after school.

**13. Correct the following sentence to show subject-verb agreement.**

The team are going to win the game.

Do NOT write your answers in this book. To open the answer sheet, scan the QR code or visit **lumoslearning.com/a/6e021**

## Chapter 3 → Lesson 2: Correct Use of Adjectives and Adverbs

1. **Identify the adjective in the following sentence.**

   The book that I was reading had colorful pages.

   Ⓐ colorful
   Ⓑ reading
   Ⓒ pages
   Ⓓ book

2. **Identify the adjective/adjectives in the following sentence.**

   Earth is the most beautiful planet in the solar system.

   Ⓐ Earth
   Ⓑ beautiful
   Ⓒ system
   Ⓓ planet

3. **Identify the adjective in this sentence.**

   The frightened alien ran back into its airship.

   Ⓐ airship
   Ⓑ alien
   Ⓒ frightened
   Ⓓ ran

**4. Identify the adverb in the following sentence.**

The mother was quite unhappy to see her son leave.

Ⓐ quite
Ⓑ unhappy
Ⓒ the
Ⓓ leave

**5. Identify the adverb in the following sentence.**

The long wait made him utterly tired.

Ⓐ long
Ⓑ wait
Ⓒ tired
Ⓓ utterly

**6. Identify the adverb in the following sentence and point out the verb it modifies/describes.**

My clever friend answered all the questions correctly.

Ⓐ adverb: clever ; verb: friend
Ⓑ adverb: correctly ; verb: questions
Ⓒ adverb: correctly ; verb: answered
Ⓓ adverb: clever : verb: question

**7. Identify the adverb in the following sentence.**

The girl politely asked the boy for her book back.

**8. Identify the adjective or adjectives in the following sentence.**

The polka dot umbrella protected Ted from the cold rain.

Ⓐ polka dot and protected
Ⓑ umbrella and polka dot
Ⓒ umbrella and rain
Ⓓ polka dot and cold

**9. Identify the adverb in the following sentence.**

Last night, the whole family slept soundly.

Ⓐ soundly
Ⓑ last
Ⓒ slept
Ⓓ night

**10. Identify the adverb in the following sentence.**

The computer printer hardly works.

**11. Identify the adverb in the following sentence.**

Peter is really busy.

Do NOT write your answers in this book. To open the answer sheet, scan the QR code or visit **lumoslearning.com/a/6e022**

## Chapter 3 → Lesson 3: Recognize Pronouns

1. **Choose the correct pronoun to complete the sentence.**

    I did it by _____.

    Ⓐ  me
    Ⓑ  myself
    Ⓒ  I
    Ⓓ  my

2. **Choose the correct pronoun to complete the sentence.**

    We _____ are responsible for the decorations.

    Ⓐ  us
    Ⓑ  ourselves
    Ⓒ  themselves
    Ⓓ  myself

3. **Choose the correct pronoun to complete the sentence.**

    She made up the story _____ .

    Ⓐ  himself
    Ⓑ  herself
    Ⓒ  itself
    Ⓓ  themself

**4. Choose the correct pronoun to complete the sentence.**

If a student wants to do well, _____ to get plenty of sleep.

Ⓐ you have
Ⓑ he or she has
Ⓒ you has
Ⓓ they have

**5. Choose the correct pronoun to complete the sentence.**

The best poker players can keep _____ faces from showing any reaction.

Ⓐ her
Ⓑ its
Ⓒ their
Ⓓ his

**6. Which of the following sentences can be used to replace the unclear referent in bold italics to make the meaning of the sentences clear?**

Charlie danced with his friend Carol and Sue most of the evening. *She is his girlfriend.*

Ⓐ Sue is his girlfriend.
Ⓑ He is her friend.
Ⓒ She is the girlfriend.
Ⓓ Carol is his girlfriend.

**7. Which of the following sentences can be used to replace the unclear referent in bold italics to make the meaning of the sentences clear?**

Riding without a helmet is a big risk. *This is unnecessary.*

Ⓐ They are unnecessary.
Ⓑ This risk is unnecessary.
Ⓒ It is unnecessary.
Ⓓ Riding is unnecessary.

**8. Which of the following sentences can be used to replace the unclear referent in bold italics to make the meaning of the sentences clear?**

The cat ate the goldfish before I could stop the tragedy. ***It was terrible.***

- Ⓐ They are terrible.
- Ⓑ The tragedy was terrible.
- Ⓒ The goldfish was terrible.
- Ⓓ The cat was terrible.

**9. Correct the following sentence to make the referent clear.**

Johnny is taller than Ahmed. He's grown a lot this year.

**10. Which of the following sentences can be used to replace the unclear referent in bold italics to make the meaning of the sentences clear?**

The Sharks and the Jets were the gangs in West Side Story. ***They performed great dances.***

- Ⓐ The gangs performed great dances.
- Ⓑ The sharks performed great dances.
- Ⓒ It performed great dances.
- Ⓓ The Jets performed great dances.

**11. Correct the following sentence to make the referent clear.**

Carrots are better than beets. They give you Vitamin A.

**12. Correct the following sentence to make the referent clear.**

Walking and running are more aerobic than playing team sports. They are fun, too.

Do NOT write your answers in this book. To open the answer sheet, scan the QR code or visit **lumoslearning.com/a/6e023**

## Chapter 3 → Lesson 4: Recognize and Correct Shifts in Pronoun

1. Which pronoun best completes the following sentence?

   Each student got to choose _____ own desk.

2. Which pronoun best completes the following sentences?

   All the girls were excited to be able to wear _____ new dresses to the dance.

3. Which pronoun best completes the following sentence?

   Coach Bob was proud of the way _____ team played in the game.

4. Which pronoun best completes the following sentence?

   Billy and _____ plan to ride our bikes to the park as soon as school is out.

   Ⓐ I
   Ⓑ me
   Ⓒ us
   Ⓓ his

**5. Which pronoun best completes the following sentence?**

Mrs. Marshall's students won the reading contest. _____ read more books than any other class in the sixth grade.

Ⓐ Their
Ⓑ Her
Ⓒ They
Ⓓ I

**6. Which pronoun best completes the following sentence?**

Johnny's friends are all on the football team with _____.

Ⓐ her
Ⓑ his
Ⓒ it
Ⓓ him

**7. Which pronoun best completes the following sentence?**

Lucy loves to have pepperoni and onions with extra cheese on _____ pizza.

Ⓐ her
Ⓑ their
Ⓒ his
Ⓓ my

**8. Which pronoun best completes the following sentence?**

_____ can't wait to go to see my Aunt Sara for the holidays.

Ⓐ We
Ⓑ He
Ⓒ I
Ⓓ They

**9. Which pronoun best completes the following sentence?**

When Tiffany went ice skating, _____ fell and twisted her ankle.

Ⓐ she
Ⓑ her
Ⓒ my
Ⓓ we

**10. Which pronoun best completes the following sentence?**

My dog loves playing catch with his ball, except _____ never brings it back.

Ⓐ they
Ⓑ she
Ⓒ he
Ⓓ I

Do NOT write your answers in this book. To open the answer sheet, scan the QR code or visit **lumoslearning.com/a/6e024**

## Chapter 3 → Lesson 5: Recognize and Correct Vague Pronouns

1. **Choose the pronoun that agrees with the antecedent in the following sentence.**

   He forgot _____ homework and will have detention at lunch.

   Ⓐ his
   Ⓑ my
   Ⓒ its
   Ⓓ their

2. **Choose the pronoun that agrees with the antecedent in the following sentence.**

   The students made _____ own costumes for the play.

   Ⓐ her
   Ⓑ their
   Ⓒ my
   Ⓓ our

3. **Choose the pronoun that agrees with the antecedent in the following sentence.**

   Gavin's dog follows _____ everywhere.

   Ⓐ their
   Ⓑ me
   Ⓒ his
   Ⓓ him

**4. Choose the pronoun that agrees with the antecedent in the following sentence.**

Emily and Nathan both love to sing so _____ are going to do a duet for the talent show.

Ⓐ they
Ⓑ he
Ⓒ she
Ⓓ their

**5. Choose the pronoun that agrees with the antecedent in the following sentence.**

The students practiced many hours in preparation for _____ concert.

Ⓐ their
Ⓑ there
Ⓒ our
Ⓓ his

**6. Choose the pronoun that agrees with the antecedent in the following sentence.**

Each of the students submitted _____ homework on time.

Ⓐ his or her
Ⓑ their
Ⓒ its
Ⓓ he

**7. Fill in the blank with the pronoun that agrees with the antecedent in the following sentence.**

Mary left the cookies out on the counter so I ate _____.

**8. Fill in the blank with the pronoun that agrees with the antecedent in the following sentence.**

The store was having a huge sale on all _____ shoes.

9. **Fill in the blank with the pronoun that agrees with the antecedent in the following sentence.**

   Even though Patty is packed for the trip, _____ does not feel ready to go.


10. **Choose the pronoun that agrees with the antecedent in the following sentence.**

    Billy and Luis both forgot to bring _____ sleeping bags on the camping trip.

    Ⓐ his
    Ⓑ my
    Ⓒ our
    Ⓓ their

# Chapter 3 → Lesson 6: Recognize Variations in English

1. What is the correct way to write the underlined part of the following sentence?

    Yesterday my mom baked cookies and we <u>eat</u> them all.

    Ⓐ will eat
    Ⓑ did eat
    Ⓒ eaten
    Ⓓ ate

2. What is the correct way to write the underlined part of the following sentence?

    Jenny went to the store and <u>buy</u> apples, milk, and bread.

    Ⓐ bought
    Ⓑ will buy
    Ⓒ did buy
    Ⓓ buyed

3. What is the correct way to write the underlined part of the following sentence?

    Billy and Matt rode <u>they're</u> bikes to the park.

    Ⓐ there
    Ⓑ their
    Ⓒ they
    Ⓓ them

4. **What is the correct way to write the underlined part of the following sentence?**

   My dad and I <u>builds</u> a tree house together this weekend.

   Ⓐ will build
   Ⓑ built
   Ⓒ had built
   Ⓓ build

5. **What is the correct way to write the underlined part of the following sentence?**

   They always take such good care of <u>them</u> garden.

   Ⓐ that
   Ⓑ there
   Ⓒ they're
   Ⓓ their

6. **Which of the following is an adverb that correctly fills in the blank in the sentence below?**

   She sings _____ in the choir.

   Ⓐ beautiful
   Ⓑ beautifully
   Ⓒ beautifully
   Ⓓ beauty

7. **What is the correct way to write the underlined part of the sentence?**

   Debbie always <u>did</u> her homework first thing when she gets home.

   Ⓐ does
   Ⓑ will do
   Ⓒ doesn't do
   Ⓓ didn't

8. **What is the correct way to write the underlined part of the sentence? Write your answer in the box given below.**

   Mickey's brother always takes <u>him</u> toys.

9. **What is the correct way to write the underlined part of the sentence? Write your answer in the box given below.**

   <u>Them</u> holiday lights are so pretty and sparkly.

   ☐

10. **What is the correct way to write the underlined part of the sentence? Write your answer in the box given below.**

    My dog always runs <u>happy</u> by my side.

    ☐

Do NOT write your answers in this book. To open the answer sheet, scan the QR code or visit **lumoslearning.com/a/6e026**

## Chapter 3 → Lesson 7: Demonstrate Command of Capitalization

1. **Which of the following options shows the correct capitalization for the sentence below?**

   my doctor moved to phoenix, arizona.

   Ⓐ  my doctor moved to phoenix, arizona.
   Ⓑ  My doctor moved to Phoenix, Arizona.
   Ⓒ  My doctor moved to phoenix, arizona.
   Ⓓ  My doctor moved to phoenix, arizona.

2. **Which of the following options shows the correct capitalization for the sentence below?**

   my mother called doctor billings to make an appointment for saturday.

   Ⓐ  My mother called Doctor Billings to make an appointment for Saturday.
   Ⓑ  my mother called doctor billings to make an appointment for Saturday.
   Ⓒ  My mother called doctor billings to make an appointment for saturday.
   Ⓓ  My mother called doctor Billings to make an appointment for Saturday.

3. **Which of the following options shows the correct capitalization for the sentence below?**

   mother says he is the best doctor in santa maria.

   Ⓐ  Mother says he is the best doctor in santa maria.
   Ⓑ  Mother says he is the best doctor in Santa maria.
   Ⓒ  Mother says he is the best doctor in Santa Maria.
   Ⓓ  mother says he is the best Doctor in Santa maria.

**4. Which of the following options shows the correct capitalization for the sentence below?**

the principal made pablo captain of the safety patrol.

Ⓐ The principal made pablo captain of the safety patrol.
Ⓑ The principal made Pablo Captain of the Safety Patrol.
Ⓒ The principal made pablo captain of the Safety Patrol.
Ⓓ The principal made Pablo captain of the safety patrol.

**5. Which of the following options shows the correct capitalization for the sentence below?**

captain jones of the american legion spoke at martin luther king, jr. elementary school.

Ⓐ Captain Jones of the American Legion spoke at Martin Luther King, Jr. Elementary School.
Ⓑ Captain jones of the american legion spoke at martin luther king, jr. elementary school.
Ⓒ Captain jones of the American Legion spoke at martin luther king, jr. elementary school.
Ⓓ Captain jones of the American legion spoke at Martin luther king, Jr. elementary school.

**6. Which of the following options shows the correct capitalization for the sentence below?**

dad, can you help me for a minute?

Ⓐ dad, can you help me for a minute?
Ⓑ Dad, Can You help Me for a Minute?
Ⓒ Dad, can you help me for a Minute?
Ⓓ Dad, can you help me for a minute?

**7. Which of the following options shows the correct capitalization for the sentence below?**

mom said angela can spend the night on friday.

Ⓐ Mom said angela can spend the night on friday.
Ⓑ Mom said Angela can spend the night on Friday.
Ⓒ Mom said Angela can spend the night on friday.
Ⓓ Mom said Angela can spend the Night on friday.

**8. Which of the following options shows the correct capitalization for the sentence below?**

my grandma made a german chocolate cake for sunday dinner.

Ⓐ My grandma made a german chocolate cake for sunday dinner.
Ⓑ My Grandma made a german chocolate cake for sunday dinner.
Ⓒ My grandma made a German chocolate cake for Sunday dinner.
Ⓓ my grandma made a german chocolate cake for Sunday dinner.

**9. Which of the following options shows the correct capitalization for the sentence below?**

kathy barrett lives on stanley street next door to domino's pizza.

Ⓐ Kathy Barrett lives on Stanley Street next door to Domino's Pizza.
Ⓑ Kathy barrett lives on stanley street next door to domino's pizza.
Ⓒ Kathy Barrett lives on stanley street next door to domino's pizza.
Ⓓ Kathy barrett lives on stanley street next door to Domino's pizza.

**10. Which of the following options shows the correct capitalization for the sentence below?**

michael read the call of the wild in july.

Ⓐ michael read the call of the wild in July.
Ⓑ Michael read The Call of the Wild in July.
Ⓒ Michael read the call of the wild in july.
Ⓓ Michael read The call of the wild in july.

**11. Read the below sentence and rewrite it with correct placement of capital letters.**

Mike was born in New jersey on september 13th.

**12. Read the below sentence and rewrite it with correct placement of capital letters.**

i live in malibu, california.

**13. Read the below sentence and rewrite it with correct placement of capital letters.**

In italy, the italian bread tastes very good.

Do NOT write your answers in this book. To open the answer sheet, scan the QR code or visit **lumoslearning.com/a/6e027**

## Chapter 3 → Lesson 8: Demonstrate Command of Punctuation

1. Choose the answer with the correct punctuation for the sentence below.

   Hi, Mom I'm home called Robby as he walked through the door

   Ⓐ "Hi, Mom! I'm home," called Robby as he walked through the door.
   Ⓑ Hi, Mom I'm home called Robby as he walked through the door.
   Ⓒ Hi Mom I'm home, called Robby as he walked through the door.
   Ⓓ Hi Mom, I'm home, called Robby, as he walked through the door.

2. Choose the answer with the correct punctuation for the sentence below.

   I had bananas oranges and cherries in the refrigerator but they're all gone

   Ⓐ I had bananas oranges and cherries in the refrigerator but they're all gone.
   Ⓑ I had bananas oranges and cherries in the refrigerator, but they're all gone.
   Ⓒ I had bananas, oranges, and cherries in the refrigerator, but they're all gone.
   Ⓓ I had bananas oranges and cherries, in the refrigerator, but they're all gone.

3. Choose the answer with the correct punctuation for the sentence below.

   September is the busiest month of the year that's why it's my favorite

   Ⓐ September is the busiest month of the year; that's why it's my favorite.
   Ⓑ September is the busiest month of the year that's why it's my favorite.
   Ⓒ September, is the busiest month of the year, that's why it's my favorite.
   Ⓓ September is the busiest month of the year that's why it's my favorite!

**4. Choose the answer with the correct punctuation for the sentence below.**

Which one is Olivias jacket the teacher asked

Ⓐ Which one is Olivias jacket the teacher asked?
Ⓑ Which one is Olivia's jacket the teacher asked.
Ⓒ "Which one is Olivia's jacket?" the teacher asked.
Ⓓ Which one is Olivia's jacket the teacher asked!

**5. Choose the answer with the correct punctuation for the sentence below.**

New Years Day will be on January 1 2012

Ⓐ New Years Day will be on January 1 2012.
Ⓑ New Year's Day will be on January 1, 2012.
Ⓒ New Years Day will be on January, 1, 2012.
Ⓓ New Year's Day, will be on January 1, 2012.

**6. Choose the answer with the correct punctuation for the sentence below.**

I got into a great college which made my mom happy.

Ⓐ I got in, to a great college which made, my mom happy.
Ⓑ I got in to a great, college which made my mom, happy.
Ⓒ I got into a great college, which made my mom happy.
Ⓓ I got into a great college which, made my mom happy.

**7. Choose the answer with the correct punctuation for the sentence below.**

Joyce remembered to bring her bathing suit on vacation but she left her sun screen in Dallas Texas.

Ⓐ Joyce remembered to bring her bathing suit on vacation, but she left her sun screen in Dallas, Texas.
Ⓑ Joyce remembered to bring her bathing suit on vacation but she left her sun screen in Dallas, Texas.
Ⓒ Joyce remembered to bring her bathing suit on vacation, but she left her sun screen in Dallas Texas.
Ⓓ Joyce remembered to bring her bathing suit, on vacation, but she left her sun screen, in Dallas, Texas.

**8. Choose the answer with the correct punctuation for the sentence below.**

Have you ever been to Albany New York, or Flourtown Pennsylvania.

Ⓐ  Have you ever been to Albany, New York, or Flourtown Pennsylvania?
Ⓑ  Have you ever been to Albany, New York or Flourtown, Pennsylvania.
Ⓒ  Have you ever been to Albany New York, or Flourtown, Pennsylvania.
Ⓓ  Have you ever been to Albany, New York or Flourtown, Pennsylvania?

**9. Choose the answer with the correct punctuation for the sentence below.**

Ryan stated "you shouldnt bully other kids.

Ⓐ  Ryan stated, you shouldn't bully other kids.
Ⓑ  Ryan stated, "you shouldnt bully other kids"
Ⓒ  Ryan stated, "you shouldnt bully other kids.
Ⓓ  Ryan stated, "You shouldn't bully other kids."

**10. Rewrite the sentence below with correct punctuation.**

Michelle made pizza grilled cheese and tacos for lunch but she didnt realize it was only 10:00 a.m.

**11. Rewrite the sentence below with correct punctuation.**

The teacher said "lets read the poem now.

**12. Rewrite the sentence below with correct punctuation.**

My brother whispered its a surprise.

Do NOT write your answers in this book. To open the answer sheet, scan the QR code or visit **lumoslearning.com/a/6e028**

## Chapter 3 → Lesson 9: Correct Spelling

1. **Choose the appropriate word from the following to fill in the blank.**

   Grind the wheat to a powdery _____.

   Ⓐ flower
   Ⓑ flour
   Ⓒ floor
   Ⓓ floure

2. **Choose the appropriate word from the following to fill in the blank.**

   Among all _____, my favorite is the pink rose.

   Ⓐ floors
   Ⓑ flour
   Ⓒ flowers
   Ⓓ floures

3. **Choose the appropriate word from the following to fill in the blank.**

   The last _____ creaked as I stepped on to it.

   Ⓐ stare
   Ⓑ stair
   Ⓒ steer
   Ⓓ stiar

**4. Choose the appropriate word from the following to fill in the blank.**

He _____ the ball and it flew forward.

Ⓐ through
Ⓑ threw
Ⓒ throw
Ⓓ any of the above

**5. Select the appropriate set of words, in the correct order, to fill in the blanks in the sentence below.**

I am _____ fed up by all the noise in the city, and hence am heading to the countryside for some peace and _____.

Ⓐ quiet, quite
Ⓑ quite, quiet
Ⓒ quite, quite
Ⓓ quiet, quiet

**6. Choose the correctly spelled word to fill in the blank in the sentence below.**

Britney _____ a car for her 18th birthday.

Ⓐ received
Ⓑ recieved
Ⓒ purschesed
Ⓓ baught

**7. Choose the correctly spelled word to fill in the blank in the sentence below.**

The boy was very _____ about King Tut and Egypt.

Ⓐ nowledgeable
Ⓑ knowlegeable
Ⓒ knowledgeable
Ⓓ knoledgable

**8. Choose the correctly spelled word to fill in the blank in the sentence below.**

The black and white cat had really long _____.

Ⓐ whiskers
Ⓑ whisckers
Ⓒ wisikers
Ⓓ None of the above

**9. Choose the correctly spelled word to fill in the blank in the sentence below.**

My favorite_____ is a small Italian place on Elm Street.

Ⓐ restrant
Ⓑ resturannt
Ⓒ restaurant
Ⓓ restraent

**10. Choose the correctly spelled word to fill in the blank in the sentence below.**

The _____ of the school gave a student detention.

Ⓐ principle
Ⓑ princapal
Ⓒ principel
Ⓓ principal

**11. What do you call an instrument with which you can see far away objects in the sky?**

_____

**12. What do you call a proposed route of travel and a guidebook for a journey?**

_____

Do NOT write your answers in this book. To open the answer sheet, scan the QR code or visit **lumoslearning.com/a/6e029**

## Chapter 3 → Lesson 10: Vary Sentences

1. **Select the option that best combines the given sentences.**

   The oven temperature was too hot. The cookies got burnt.

   Ⓐ  The oven temperature was too hot, the cookies got burnt.
   Ⓑ  The oven temperature was too hot because the cookies got burnt.
   Ⓒ  The oven temperature was too hot the cookies got burnt.
   Ⓓ  The oven temperature was too hot, so the cookies got burnt.

2. **Select the option that best combines the given sentences.**

   Mike and Johnny wanted to play outside. It was raining so they couldn't.

   Ⓐ  Mike and Johnny wanted to play outside, but it was raining.
   Ⓑ  Because of the rain, Mike and Johnny couldn't play outside.
   Ⓒ  Mike and Johnny wanted to play outside and it was raining so they couldn't.
   Ⓓ  Mike and Johnny wanted to play outside in the rain.

3. **Select the option that best combines the given sentences.**

   I would like to have pizza at my party. I would also like to have ice cream and chocolate cake.

   Ⓐ  I would like to have pizza at my party, and I would also like to have ice cream and chocolate cake.
   Ⓑ  I would like to have pizza at my party, and ice cream and chocolate cake.
   Ⓒ  I would like to have pizza, ice cream, and chocolate cake at my party.
   Ⓓ  At my party, I would like to have pizza and ice cream and chocolate cake.

**4. Select the option that best combines the given sentences.**

We should go to the mall. After school.

Ⓐ  After school, we should go to the mall.
Ⓑ  We should go to the mall, after school.
Ⓒ  We should go to the mall, and after school.
Ⓓ  After school, to the mall we should go.

**5. Select the option that best combines the given sentences.**

The cat chases the dog. The dog chases the cat.

Ⓐ  The cat chases the dog, and the dog chases the cat.
Ⓑ  The cat chases the dog, but the dog chases the cat.
Ⓒ  The cat chases the dog, the dog chases the cat.
Ⓓ  The cat and dog chase each other.

**6. Select the option that best combines the given sentences.**

Summer is nice. Spring is my favorite.

Ⓐ  Summer is nice, and spring is my favorite.
Ⓑ  Summer is nice, spring is my favorite.
Ⓒ  Summer is nice, but spring is my favorite.
Ⓓ  Summer and spring are nice.

**7. Select the option that best combines the given sentences.**

We will be going camping. After school on Friday.

Ⓐ  We will be going camping, and after school on Friday.
Ⓑ  After school on Friday, we will be going camping.
Ⓒ  After school on Friday we will be going camping.
Ⓓ  Camping we are going after school on Friday.

**8. Select the option that best combines the given sentences.**

Before the party I have to wash the dishes. I also have to do the laundry. And walk the dog.

Ⓐ  Before the party I have to wash the dishes. I also have to do the laundry and walk the dog.
Ⓑ  Before the party I have to wash the dishes do the laundry and walk the dog.
Ⓒ  Before the party, I have to wash the dishes, do the laundry and walk the dog.
Ⓓ  I have to wash the dishes. I also have to do the laundry and walk the dog. Before the party.

**9. Select the option that best combines the given sentences.**

Lisa got a book. She got it at the library.

Ⓐ  Lisa got a book at the library.
Ⓑ  Lisa got a book, and she got it at the library.
Ⓒ  Lisa got a book, so she got it at the library.
Ⓓ  At the library, Lisa got her book.

**10. Select the option that best combines the given sentences.**

The puppy was soft and cuddly. It was brown.

Ⓐ  The puppy was soft and cuddly, and it was brown.
Ⓑ  The brown puppy was soft and cuddly.
Ⓒ  The puppy was soft and cuddly and brown.
Ⓓ  The puppy was brown and it was soft and it was cuddly.

Do NOT write your answers in this book. To open the answer sheet, scan the QR code or visit *lumoslearning.com/a/6e030*

## Chapter 3 → Lesson 11: Maintain Consistency in Style and Tone

1. **Which of the following sentences is properly constructed and effectively communicates its meaning?**

   Ⓐ Even though the sun was shining, Mary couldn't help but feel chilled by the cool morning breeze.
   Ⓑ Even though the sun was shining, Mary was still cold.
   Ⓒ The sun was shining but the breeze made Mary cold.
   Ⓓ Mary was chilled on the sunny, yet breeze morning.

2. **Which of the following sentences uses the most descriptive words and style?**

   Ⓐ As the darkness fell, Scott was scared of what might be out there.
   Ⓑ As the darkness fell, Scott couldn't help but be wary of what might lurk out there in the shadows.
   Ⓒ As the darkness fell, Scott was frightened by what he could not see.
   Ⓓ Scott is scared of the dark.

3. **Which of the following sentences provides the most detail about the topic?**

   Ⓐ Callie loved the smell of cookies.
   Ⓑ Callie loved the smell of her mother's cookies.
   Ⓒ Callie loved the smell of her mother's fresh baked cookies.
   Ⓓ Callie loved the smell of her mother's fresh baked chocolate chip cookies.

4. **Which of the following sentences provides sufficient information in an efficient format?**

   Ⓐ George Washington was the first president. He was also a general in the American Revolution.
   Ⓑ George Washington was not only the first president, but he was also a general in the American Revolution.
   Ⓒ George Washington was a general and president.
   Ⓓ George Washington was the first president and a general in the American Revolution.

**5. Which of the following sentences is most concise?**

Ⓐ I loved the movie. I just didn't like the surprise ending.
Ⓑ I loved the movie, and I just didn't like the surprise ending.
Ⓒ I loved the movie, but I just didn't like the surprise ending.
Ⓓ I loved the movie, but I didn't like the surprise ending.

**6. Which of the following sentences is the most concise and accurate?**

Ⓐ I'm so nervous for the play. What if I forget my lines? What if I fall down and everyone laughs at me?
Ⓑ I'm so nervous for the play. What if I forget my lines, fall down, and everyone laughs at me?
Ⓒ I'm so nervous for the play. What if I forget my lines or fall down and everyone laughs at me?
Ⓓ I am nervous that I will forget my lines. I am nervous I will fall down and everyone will laugh at me.

**7. Which of the following sentences provides the most imaginative style?**

Ⓐ After the dog got out of the yard, Freddie ran after it.
Ⓑ The dog got out of the yard. Freddie ran after it.
Ⓒ Freddie ran after the dog, after it got out of the yard.
Ⓓ The dog got out of the yard and Freddie ran after it.

**8. Which of the following sentences provides the most detailed, concise expression of the events?**

Ⓐ Seth and Iris walked on the beach. They collected sea shells.
Ⓑ As they walked along the beach, Seth and Iris collected sea shells.
Ⓒ Seth and Iris walked and collected sea shells.
Ⓓ At the beach, Seth and Iris walked. They also collected sea shells.

**9. Which of the following sentences is the most concise?**

Ⓐ Beth thought the test was hard and difficult. Mary thought the test was easy.
Ⓑ While Beth thought the test was challenging, Mary thought it was easy.
Ⓒ Beth thought the test was hard and Mary thought it was easy.
Ⓓ Beth thought the test was hard and difficult, but Mary thought the test was easy.

**10. Which of the following sentences uses the smoothest and most concise language to describe the event?**

Ⓐ The lights slowly darkened to signal the start of the movie. Mark and Anthony got excited.
Ⓑ The lights slowly darkened to signal the start of the movie, and Mark and Anthony got excited.
Ⓒ Mark and Anthony got excited when the lights slowly darkened to signal the start of the movie.
Ⓓ The lights went out so the movie could start. Mark and Anthony got excited.

LumosLearning.com

Do NOT write your answers in this book. To open the answer sheet, scan the QR code or visit **lumoslearning.com/a/6e031**

## Chapter 3 → Lesson 12: Use Clues To Determine Multiple-meaning Words

**Question 1 is based on the passage below**

Crab and shrimp: they're not just for dinner anymore. A natural polymer found in the exoskeletons of crustaceans can keep your car cleaner. Never heard of chitosan? You may not be able to say that for long. Researchers in the School of Fashion and Textiles at RMIT are using the biopolymer, found in the exoskeletons of crustaceans such as crabs and shrimp, to coat the 100% polyester fabric used in automobiles. Combining fragrant oils with the polymer, which has the ability to form an antimicrobial film, creates a durable, fragrant finish in the fabric.

**1. Based on this passage, crabs and shrimp are _____.**

Ⓐ dinner
Ⓑ fragrant
Ⓒ crustaceans
Ⓓ polyester

**Question 2 is based on the passage below**

A natural polymer found in the exoskeletons of crustaceans can keep your car cleaner. Researchers in the School of Fashion and Textiles at RMIT are using the biopolymer, found in the exoskeletons of crustaceans such as crabs and shrimp, to coat the 100% polyester fabric used in automobiles. Combining fragrance oils with the polymer, which has the ability to form an antimicrobial film, creates a durable, fragrant finish in the fabric.

**2. Based on the prefix "exo-," and prior knowledge about crabs and shrimp, an exoskeleton is probably: _____.**

Ⓐ a skeleton that is outside the body
Ⓑ a skeleton that is inside the body
Ⓒ a soft skeleton
Ⓓ a durable skeleton

### Question 3 is based on the passage below

Crab and shrimp: they're not just for dinner anymore. A natural polymer found in the exoskeletons of crustaceans can keep your car cleaner. Never heard of chitosan? You may not be able to say that for long. Researchers in the School of Fashion and Textiles at RMIT are using the biopolymer, found in the exoskeletons of crustaceans such as crabs and shrimp, to coat the 100% polyester fabric used in automobiles. Combining fragrance oils with the polymer, which has the ability to form an antimicrobial film, creates a durable, fragrant finish in the fabric.

3. Based on the prefix "bio-," a biopolymer is probably: _____.

   Ⓐ a chemical substance found in the earth
   Ⓑ a chemical substance found in a living thing
   Ⓒ a chemical substance found in water
   Ⓓ a chemical substance found in the air

### Question 4 is based on the passage below

Researchers at RMIT's School of Fashion and Textiles are developing anti-stain, antimicrobial, and anti-odor textiles that keep car interiors clean and sweet-smelling. But that's not all they've got up their sleeves: projects range from wearable technology to protective fabrics – even sports apparel that can monitor your performance.

4. 'But that's not all they've got up their sleeves', could mean: _____.

   Ⓐ They have some more projects coming up
   Ⓑ they have no other projects coming up
   Ⓒ they have rolled up their sleeves
   Ⓓ they have projects on sleeves

### Question 5 is based on the passage below

Researchers at RMIT's School of Fashion and Textiles are developing anti-stain, antimicrobial, and anti-odor textiles that keep car interiors clean and sweet-smelling.

5. Anti-odor and sweet-smelling textiles are _____.

   Ⓐ stainless
   Ⓑ fragrant
   Ⓒ durable
   Ⓓ smelly

### Question 6 is based on the passage below

My friends and I were up early that spring morning. We were going hiking up in the cliffs. We were hiking for 4 days and 3 nights. I was very excited about this trip because we were going to stay in log cabins built on huge strong trees and cliffs. These trees and cliffs were very old and housed a lot of animals and birds.

We began the first day of our hiking at the main office, and our captain briefed us about the trails we were taking and the things we could see and hear.

The first trail was called the "aerie" trail. It was called so because the cliffs here were very high and housed a lot of eagles' nests (called aeries). We started our hike at 9:00 am and reached our first log cabin destination at around 6:00 pm. The cabin was large and airy. It was very refreshing to see these cabins and the beds. Once up in my cabin I sat on my bed and looked out the window. It was a sight to behold! From my window, I could see lots of aeries at the cliff tops. I could also see little baby eagles inside these aeries. One of them was so close that I could see about 3 baby eagles inside the nest. I moved close to the window and fell asleep watching these tiny little birds.

**6. In the above passage, what is the synonym for the word "housed"?**

Ⓐ attracted
Ⓑ held
Ⓒ accepted
Ⓓ none of the above

### Question 7 is based on the passage below

When Westinghouse, the inventor of the air brake was working on his great invention, he made an application for a trial of his device on the New York Central Railroad.

**7. Choose the meaning of the word "brake" according to the above sentence.**

Ⓐ a weapon
Ⓑ an instrument
Ⓒ a mechanical device which makes a vehicle stop when pressed
Ⓓ the pedal

**8. Which of the following sets contains antonyms?**

Ⓐ return, march
Ⓑ alive, dead
Ⓒ opened, broke
Ⓓ collect, take

**9. The volume of traffic was high on the interstate.**
   **In the above sentence, the meaning of volume is _____.**

   Ⓐ a unit of written material assembled together
   Ⓑ loudness of sound
   Ⓒ a roll of parchment
   Ⓓ the amount of space occupied

**10. The money in my savings account is earning some interest.**
   **In the above sentence, the meaning of interest is _____.**

   Ⓐ a state of curiosity
   Ⓑ attention to something
   Ⓒ an extra amount
   Ⓓ a charge for a loan

**11. Which of the following sets contains antonyms?**

   Ⓐ Accept, take
   Ⓑ Ancient, modern
   Ⓒ argue, disagree
   Ⓓ Arrive, come

**12. Which of the following sets contains antonyms?**

   Ⓐ Blunt, sharp
   Ⓑ Careful, caring
   Ⓒ Cold, cool
   Ⓓ Dirty, gross

**13. Which of the following sets contains antonyms?**

   Ⓐ Cheap, poor
   Ⓑ Early, awake
   Ⓒ Domestic, foreign
   Ⓓ East, north

Do NOT write your answers in this book. To open the answer sheet, scan the QR code or visit **lumoslearning.com/a/6e032**

## Chapter 3 → Lesson 13: Use Context Clues to Determine Word Meaning

**Question 1 is based on the context below**

Julio was happy and astounded when he won MVP for the soccer season. He had been sure that Reuben or Carlos were going to be chosen.

**1. The word "astounded" in this context means: _____.**

- Ⓐ disappointed
- Ⓑ very surprised
- Ⓒ satisfied
- Ⓓ pleased

**Question 2 is based on the context below**

A spider web may look flimsy, but spider silk is actually five times stronger than steel. It is tougher, stronger, and more flexible than anything humans have been able to produce.

**2. The word "flimsy" in this context means: _____.**

- Ⓐ beautiful
- Ⓑ silky
- Ⓒ weak
- Ⓓ inflexible

### Question 3 is based on the context below

New Jersey is on the east coast of the Mid-Atlantic region of the United States of America. It is bordered by the Atlantic Ocean to the east and by Delaware to the southwest, Pennsylvania to the west, and New York to the north and northeast. Parts of the state are suburbs of New York City, just across the Hudson River to the northeast, and Philadelphia, just across the Delaware River on the southwest.

**3. In the above context, "bordered" means _____.**

- Ⓐ surrounded by
- Ⓑ marked by
- Ⓒ differentiated by
- Ⓓ separated by

### Question 4 is based on the context below

Africa is a very diverse continent, with each country, or even each part of a country, having its own unique culture. While it is common for people in the West to refer to Africa as if it was a single country, one should remember the sheer size of the continent. Africa is not one country but 55 different countries, meaning that it is impossible to make generalizations about Africa as a whole.

**4. In the above context, "sheer" means _____.**

- Ⓐ vast
- Ⓑ transparent
- Ⓒ unmixed
- Ⓓ small

### Question 5 is based on the context below

My dog is devoted to my family. He would never leave us.

**5. In the above context, "devoted" means _____**

- Ⓐ loyal
- Ⓑ loving
- Ⓒ unloving
- Ⓓ hated

### Question 6 is based on the context below

It is always beneficial to eat your vegetables. That's why your doctor tells you to eat plenty of fruits and vegetables.

**6. In the above context, "beneficial" means _____**

- Ⓐ horrible
- Ⓑ wrong
- Ⓒ good for you
- Ⓓ nice

### Question 7 is based on the context below

The stench coming from the garbage can was unbearable.

**7. In the above context, "stench" means _____**

- Ⓐ sugary
- Ⓑ freshness
- Ⓒ sweetness
- Ⓓ stink

### Question 8 is based on the context below

The celebrity walked the red carpet and was overwhelmed by the barrage of questions from reporters.

**8. In the above context, "barrage" means _____**

- Ⓐ abundance
- Ⓑ few
- Ⓒ twenty
- Ⓓ little

**Question 9 is based on the context below**

The sweltering summer heat made the beach unpleasant.

**9. In the above context, "sweltering" means _____**

- Ⓐ cold
- Ⓑ frigid
- Ⓒ hot
- Ⓓ humid

**Question 10 is based on the context below**

The big, nasty creature was brown and hairy; it looked hideous.

**10. In the above context, "hideous" means _____**

**Question 11 is based on the context below**

Jon was reluctant to see the horror movie because he did not like scary things.

**11. In the above context, 'reluctant' means _____**

**Question 12 is based on the context below**

The clothes were saturated because they were left outside in the rain.

**12. In the above context, 'saturated' means _____**

## Chapter 3 → Lesson 14: Use Common Roots and Affixes

1. Which of the following is a true statement?

   Ⓐ A suffix or ending is an affix, which is placed at the end of a word.
   Ⓑ A prefix or beginning is an affix, which is placed at the beginning of a word.
   Ⓒ A suffix is attached at the beginning of the word.
   Ⓓ Both A and B

2. What does the word that results from adding the suffix "able" to the word "cap" mean?

   Ⓐ able to do something
   Ⓑ to do anything
   Ⓒ not able to do something
   Ⓓ All of the above

3. Identify the suffix in the following words:

   Salvage, Storage, Forage

   Ⓐ A
   Ⓑ ge
   Ⓒ age
   Ⓓ rage

4. Identify the prefix in the following words.

   Anarchy, Anonymous, Anemia

   Ⓐ Anna
   Ⓑ An
   Ⓒ Ana
   Ⓓ Both A and B

**5. What does the suffix "less" mean?**

Ⓐ Too little
Ⓑ With
Ⓒ Without
Ⓓ None of the above

**6. What does the suffix "ology" mean?**

Ⓐ Study
Ⓑ Vocabulary
Ⓒ Sadness
Ⓓ Study of animals

**7. Identify the meaning of the root word in the following words:**

Commemorate, Commune, Community

---

**8. Which of the following statements is true?**

Ⓐ The first rule of decoding words is to find out if the word has any suffixes or prefixes
Ⓑ You should always divide between the consonants
Ⓒ Both A and B
Ⓓ None of the above

**9. Using the rule 'divide between the consonants', decode the word 'sentence'.**

Ⓐ se-n-tence
Ⓑ sen-tence
Ⓒ sen-ten-ce
Ⓓ none of the above

**10. What is the correct way to decode the word 'Monarch'**

Ⓐ mona-rch
Ⓑ mon-ar-ch
Ⓒ mon-a-rch
Ⓓ mon-arch

**11. Identify the prefix in the following words:**

Diameter, diagnol, diabolical

**12. Identify the meaning of the root word in the following words:**

Recede, secede, precede

Do NOT write your answers in this book. To open the answer sheet, scan the QR code or visit **lumoslearning.com/a/6e034**

## Chapter 3 → Lesson 15: Consult Reference Materials

1. Select the option in which the given words are alphabetized properly (alphabetize means to rearrange the words in the order that they would appear in a dictionary).

   hibiscus, petunia, rose, honeysuckle, daffodil

   Ⓐ hibiscus, petunia, rose, honeysuckle, daffodil
   Ⓑ daffodil, hibiscus, honeysuckle, petunia, rose
   Ⓒ daffodil, honeysuckle, hibiscus, petunia, rose
   Ⓓ hibiscus, petunia, rose, daffodil, honeysuckle

2. Select the option in which the given words are alphabetized properly (alphabetize means to rearrange the words in the order that they would appear in a dictionary)

   mouse, mule, monkey, moose, mole

   Ⓐ mouse, monkey, moose, mole, mule
   Ⓑ mouse, mule, monkey, moose, mole
   Ⓒ mouse, moose, monkey, mole, mule
   Ⓓ mole, monkey, moose, mouse, mule

3. Select the option in which the given words are alphabetized properly (alphabetize means to rearrange the words in the order that they would appear in a dictionary)

   sustain, solicit, sizzle, sanitize, secure

   Ⓐ sustain, solicit, sizzle, sanitize, secure
   Ⓑ sanitize, secure, sustain, solicit, sizzle
   Ⓒ sanitize, solicit, sizzle, sustain, secure
   Ⓓ sanitize, secure, sizzle, solicit, sustain

**4. The dictionary contains _____.**

Ⓐ meaning of a word
Ⓑ pronunciation of a word
Ⓒ the etymology (where the word came from)
Ⓓ all the above

**5. Which of the following answer choices can you find in a thesaurus?**

Ⓐ homonym
Ⓑ homograph
Ⓒ synonym
Ⓓ definition

**6. How do you go about looking up a word in the dictionary?**

Ⓐ Open the dictionary.
Ⓑ Open the dictionary to the page that has the first two letters of the word you are looking for.
Ⓒ Open the dictionary to the page that has the last two letters of the word.
Ⓓ Open the dictionary and look in the table of contents.

**7. What are guidewords in a dictionary?**

Ⓐ Guidewords are words that tell you how to pronounce your word
Ⓑ Guidewords are located at the bottom of each page
Ⓒ Guidewords are words that tell you the part of speech of your word
Ⓓ Guidewords are at the top of each page to tell you the first and last words you will find on that page.

**8. How many syllables are in the word "organized?"**

**9. How many syllables are in the word "jacket?"**

Ⓐ 1
Ⓑ 3
Ⓒ 2
Ⓓ 4

10. How many syllables would you have, if you divide the word 'hyacinth'?
   Ⓐ 2
   Ⓑ 3
   Ⓒ 8
   Ⓓ 4

11. Alphabetize the following words as they are found in a dictionary and write it in the correct sequence in the boxes given below:

   obscure, obsess, obligation, objective

   ◯  ◯  ◯  ◯

12. Alphabetize the following words as they are found in a dictionary and write it in the correct sequence in the boxes given below:

   hesitate, hence, hibernate, hero

   ◯  ◯  ◯  ◯

Do NOT write your answers in this book. To open the answer sheet, scan the QR code or visit **lumoslearning.com/a/6e035**

## Chapter 3 → Lesson 16: Determine the Meaning of a Word

1. What does the underlined word in the sentence mean?

   Johnny was certain he hadn't <u>misplaced</u> his glove but he couldn't find it.

   Ⓐ found
   Ⓑ lost
   Ⓒ hid
   Ⓓ borrowed

2. What does the underlined word in the sentence mean?

   Despite the <u>brisk</u> temperatures, football fans still packed the stadium to watch the championship game.

   Ⓐ hot
   Ⓑ fast
   Ⓒ cool
   Ⓓ exciting

3. What does the underlined word in the sentence mean?

   Natalie and Sophia couldn't wait to ride the roller coaster. They'd heard it was very <u>exhilarating</u>.

   Ⓐ fast
   Ⓑ frightening
   Ⓒ exciting
   Ⓓ boring

**4. What does the underlined word in the sentence mean?**

Billy always found raking leaves to be a very <u>mundane</u> chore. It was the same thing over and over.

Ⓐ fun
Ⓑ challenging
Ⓒ easy
Ⓓ boring

**5. What does the underlined word in the sentence mean?**

The whimpering puppies were clearly <u>ravenous</u>. They devoured the food when it was ready.

Ⓐ hungry
Ⓑ sleepy
Ⓒ playful
Ⓓ scared

**6. What does the underlined word in the sentence mean?**

The basketball team had <u>triumphed</u> over their opponents.

Ⓐ lost
Ⓑ forfeited
Ⓒ competed
Ⓓ won

**7. What does the underlined word in the sentence mean?**

Abby found the new student to be <u>bewitching</u>.

Ⓐ scary
Ⓑ charming
Ⓒ kind
Ⓓ boring

**8. What does the underlined word in the sentence mean?**

Julia found fishing to be completely <u>repulsing</u>. She wanted nothing to do with putting the worm on the hook.

Ⓐ wonderful
Ⓑ delightful
Ⓒ relaxing
Ⓓ awful

**9. What does the underlined word in the sentence mean?**

As Tony and Steve climbed higher and higher up the mountainside, they noticed everything took on a whole new <u>perspective</u>.

Ⓐ appearance
Ⓑ experience
Ⓒ height
Ⓓ altitude

**10. If you do not know what a word means, where can you look?**

Ⓐ Dictionary
Ⓑ Thesaurus
Ⓒ Glossary
Ⓓ All of the above

Do NOT write your answers in this book. To open the answer sheet, scan the QR code or visit **lumoslearning.com/a/6e036**

# Chapter 3 → Lesson 17: Interpret Figures of Speech

1. What type of figurative language is used in the sentence below?

    Jimmy and Johnny jumped like jelly beans.

    Ⓐ Metaphor
    Ⓑ Idiom
    Ⓒ Personification
    Ⓓ Alliteration

2. What type of figurative language is being used in the sentence below?

    Don't spill the beans.

    Ⓐ Idiom
    Ⓑ Onomatopoeia
    Ⓒ Personification
    Ⓓ Alliteration

3. What type of figurative language is being used in the sentence below?

    That sandwich is as big as a car.

    Ⓐ Personification
    Ⓑ Simile
    Ⓒ Metaphor
    Ⓓ Alliteration

**4. What type of figurative language is being used in the sentence below?**

We better cook a lot of food; we have an army to feed.

Ⓐ Hyperbole
Ⓑ Alliteration
Ⓒ Idiom
Ⓓ Personification

**5. What type of figurative language is being used in the sentence below?**

The baby bear looked up at its mother with adoring eyes filled with love.

Ⓐ Idiom
Ⓑ Alliteration
Ⓒ Personification
Ⓓ Metaphor

**6. What type of figurative language is being used in the sentence below?**

Zoom, roared the car engine.

Ⓐ Personification
Ⓑ Simile
Ⓒ Idiom
Ⓓ Onomatopoeia

**7. What type of figurative language is being used in the sentence below?**

Katy is a pig when she eats.

Ⓐ Simile
Ⓑ Metaphor
Ⓒ Onomatopoeia
Ⓓ Alliteration

**8. What type of figurative language is being used in the sentence below?**

Yesterday was the worst day of my entire life.

Ⓐ Alliteration
Ⓑ Hyperbole
Ⓒ Idiom
Ⓓ Simile

**9. What type of figurative language is being used in the sentence below? Enter your answer in the box given below**

Stop pulling my leg.

_____

**10. What type of figurative language is being used in the sentence below? Enter your answer in the box given below**

Danielle's dancing is as graceful as a swan.

_____

**11. Match the figure of speech with its example**

( The fire swallowed the entire forest )    ( He is as cunning as a fox )    ( The world is a stage )

simile

Metaphor

Personification

Do NOT write your answers in this book. To open the answer sheet, scan the QR code or visit **lumoslearning.com/a/6e037**

## Chapter 3 → Lesson 18: Use Relationships to Better Understand Words

1. **Identify the cause and the effect in the following sentence:**

   The blizzard was so widespread that all flights were cancelled.

   cause _____ effect _____

   Ⓐ cause-blizzard; effect- flights cancelled
   Ⓑ cause-flights; effect- blizzard
   Ⓒ cause-blizzard; effect- flights
   Ⓓ cause-cancelled flights; effect- widespread blizzard

2. **Identify the cause and the effect in the following sentence:**

   Several hundred people were left homeless by the flood.

   cause _____ effect _____

   Ⓐ cause- homeless people; effect -flood
   Ⓑ cause- flood; effect - people left homeless
   Ⓒ cause- people; effect -homeless
   Ⓓ cause- flood; effect -several hundred people

**3. Identify the cause and the effect in the following sentence:**

Pedro's friendly attitude got him the job.

cause _____ effect _____

Ⓐ cause- Pedro; effect- friendly attitude
Ⓑ cause- Pedro; effect- got the job
Ⓒ cause- friendly attitude; effect- got the job
Ⓓ cause- job; effect- friendly attitude

**4. Choose the correct animal which belongs to the category of mammals:** _____

Ⓐ giraffe
Ⓑ cheese
Ⓒ frogs
Ⓓ bees

**5. Choose the correct item which belongs to the category of birds:** _____

Ⓐ parrots
Ⓑ giraffes
Ⓒ bees
Ⓓ sharks

**6. Choose the correct item which belongs to the category of desserts:** _____

Ⓐ elephants
Ⓑ pie
Ⓒ carrots
Ⓓ cheese

7. **This exercise will help you practice identifying parts and wholes. Arrange the following words in order by size:**

   galaxy, universe, county, country, town, neighborhood, state, world, continent, solar system, hemisphere.

   A street is part of a _____,
   which is part of a _____,
   which is part of a _____,
   which is part of a _____,
   which is part of a _____,
   which is part of a _____,
   which is part of a _____,
   which is part of a _____,
   which is part of a _____,
   which is part of a _____,
   which is part of a _____,
   which is part of a _____.

   Ⓐ town; neighborhood; county; state; country; continent; galaxy; hemisphere; world; universe; solar system
   Ⓑ world; solar system; galaxy; universe; neighborhood; town; county; state; country; continent; hemisphere;
   Ⓒ neighborhood; town; county; state; country; continent; hemisphere; world; solar system; galaxy; universe
   Ⓓ neighborhood; galaxy; universe; town; county; state; country; hemisphere; world; solar system; continent

8. **Choose the correct item which belongs to the category of insects:** _____

   Ⓐ sharks
   Ⓑ bees
   Ⓒ frogs
   Ⓓ parrots

**9. Identify the cause and the effect in the following sentence:**

The burned popcorn made the whole house smell like smoke.

cause _____ effect _____

Ⓐ cause-popcorn; effect- smoke
Ⓑ cause- burned popcorn; effect- smoky smell
Ⓒ cause-house; effect- burned popcorn
Ⓓ cause-smoky smell; effect- burned popcorn

**10. Identify the cause and the effect in the following sentence:**

He practiced until he could make 3 out of 4 free throws.

cause _____ effect _____

Ⓐ cause- free throws; effect-practice
Ⓑ cause- practice; effect- four free throws
Ⓒ cause- practice; effect- make three out of four free throws
Ⓓ cause- free throws; effect- three throws

**11. Identify the cause and the effect in the following sentence:**

The evenings are longer during Daylight Saving Time.

cause _____ effect _____

**12. Identify the cause and the effect in the following sentence:**

Whistling while you work makes the task easier.

cause _____ effect _____

**13. Identify the cause and the effect in the following sentence:**

The street sweeper makes a lot of noise.

cause _____ effect _____

Do NOT write your answers in this book. To open the answer sheet, scan the QR code or visit **lumoslearning.com/a/6e038**

## Chapter 3 → Lesson 19: Distinguish Between Word Associations and Definitions

1. **Denotation of a word is the _____.**

   Ⓐ slang for a word
   Ⓑ literal meaning
   Ⓒ part of speech of a word
   Ⓓ feelings we have about a word

2. **Connotation refers to _____.**

   Ⓐ the literal meaning of a word
   Ⓑ the part of speech of a word
   Ⓒ how we feel about a word
   Ⓓ the slang meaning of a word

3. **Which of the following words has the same denotative meaning as the word house?**

   Ⓐ dwelling
   Ⓑ abode
   Ⓒ residence
   Ⓓ All of the above

4. **Which of the following words has the same denotative meaning as the word child?**

   Ⓐ elderly
   Ⓑ ancient
   Ⓒ adolescent
   Ⓓ None of the above

5. Which of the following words have the same denotation?

   Ⓐ smelly; smiley
   Ⓑ sweet; sweat
   Ⓒ trash; garbage
   Ⓓ stubborn; easy-going

6. Which of the following words have the same denotation?

   Ⓐ expensive; cheap
   Ⓑ short; tall
   Ⓒ rabbit; horse
   Ⓓ curious; nosy

The word "inexpensive" has a positive connotation.

7. Which of the following words has the same denotation but a negative connotation?

   Ⓐ costly
   Ⓑ expensive
   Ⓒ free
   Ⓓ cheap

8. Which of the following words has a negative connotation?

   Ⓐ Creative
   Ⓑ Innovative
   Ⓒ Cunning
   Ⓓ Resourceful

9. Which of the following words has a neutral connotation?

   Ⓐ Skinny
   Ⓑ Thin
   Ⓒ Slim
   Ⓓ Lean

The word "old" has a negative connotation.

10. Which of the following words has the same denotation but a positive connotation?

   Ⓐ Decrepit
   Ⓑ Ancient
   Ⓒ Elderly
   Ⓓ Over the hill

LumosLearning.com

Do NOT write your answers in this book. To open the answer sheet, scan the QR code or visit **lumoslearning.com/a/6e039**

# Chapter 3 → Lesson 20: Use Grade Appropriate Words

The word "racket" has multiple meanings.

**1. Which sentence below correctly uses the word "racket" to mean "noise"?**

- Ⓐ I nearly forgot my racket before tennis practice.
- Ⓑ There was a lot of racket coming from my brother's room.
- Ⓒ My racket broke when I dropped it down the stairs.
- Ⓓ I hope I get a new racket for my birthday.

The word "bear" has multiple meanings.

**2. Which sentence below correctly uses the word "bear" to mean "to hold up"?**

- Ⓐ The baby bear is so cute!
- Ⓑ I cannot bear to see someone hurt.
- Ⓒ That apple tree sure does bear a lot of fruit.
- Ⓓ I can't bear to stand on my broken ankle.

The word "patient" has multiple meanings.

**3. Which sentence below correctly uses the word "patient" to mean "quietly waiting"?**

- Ⓐ The doctor sent the patient for x-rays of her wrist.
- Ⓑ The nurse checked on the patient frequently.
- Ⓒ The little boy is being very patient in line.
- Ⓓ The patient needs to go home and rest before he feels better.

The word "pound" has multiple meanings.

**4. Which sentence below correctly uses the word "pound" to mean "to hit"?**

Ⓐ We got our new dog from the pound.
Ⓑ Jimmy had to pound on the box to get it to break open.
Ⓒ The watermelon weighs 16 pounds!
Ⓓ Sixteen ounces is equal to one pound.

The word "pack" has multiple meanings.

**5. Which sentence uses the word "pack" where it means "a group of animals?"**

Ⓐ Did you see that pack of wolves down in the valley?
Ⓑ Don't forget to pack your toothbrush.
Ⓒ I packed a sandwich, an apple, and a cookie in your lunch.
Ⓓ Marissa put her pack on her back.

**6. Which of the following words best complete the sentence?**

Even though I studied, I feel very _____ about the test in Science.

Ⓐ excited
Ⓑ anxious
Ⓒ happy
Ⓓ ready

**7. Which of the following words best completes the sentence?**

I can't believe how _____ the Grand Canyon is.

Ⓐ immense
Ⓑ small
Ⓒ brown
Ⓓ stationary

LumosLearning.com

8. Which of the following words best completes the sentence?

They say the race is very _____ , so I had better spend some extra time training.

- Ⓐ easy
- Ⓑ smooth
- Ⓒ distinct
- Ⓓ rigorous

9. Which of the following words best completes the sentence?

Joey got himself into quite a _____ when he cheated on the test.

- Ⓐ predicament
- Ⓑ problem
- Ⓒ challenge
- Ⓓ bit of luck

10. Which of the following words best completes the sentence?

The team was very _____ about practicing.

- Ⓐ lazy
- Ⓑ sloppy
- Ⓒ successful
- Ⓓ diligent

# End of Language

# Notes

**Test Mastery tedBook by Lumos Learning - 6th Grade English Language Arts State (ELA) Test Prep Workbook | Two Online Grade 6 ELA Practice Tests & Learning Resources: Covers Reading: Literature, Reading: Informational Text, and Language (Ages 11-12)**

Contributing Author - Heather Dorey
Contributing Author - Janet Redell
Contributing Author - George Smith
Executive Producer - Mukunda Krishnaswamy
Program Director - Anirudh Agarwal
Designer and Illustrator - Sowmya R.

**COPYRIGHT ©2023 by Lumos Information Services, LLC.** ALL RIGHTS RESERVED. No portion of this book may be reproduced mechanically, electronically or by any other means, including photocopying, recording, taping, Web Distribution or Information Storage and Retrieval systems, without prior written permission of the Publisher, Lumos Information Services, LLC.

**ISBN 13: 978-1959697589**

**Printed in the United States of America**

## CONTACT INFORMATION

**LUMOS INFORMATION SERVICES, LLC**

 PO Box 1575, Piscataway, NJ 08855-1575
 www.LumosLearning.com

Email: support@lumoslearning.com
Tel: (732) 384-0146
Fax: (866) 283-6471

# What if I buy more than one Lumos tedBook?

**Step 1** → **Visit the link given below and login to your parent/teacher account**

www.lumoslearning.com

**Step 2** → Go to the **"My tedBooks"** section and place the book access code and submit (See the first page for access code).

**Step 3** → **Add the new book**

To add the new book for a registered student, choose the '**Student**' button and click on submit.

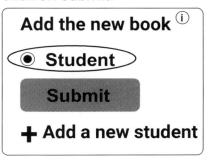

To add the new book for a new student, choose the '**Add New Student**' button and complete the student registration.

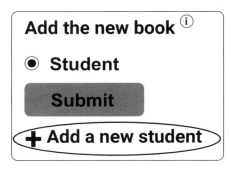

LumosLearning.com

# Also Available

Test Mastery tedBook by Lumos Learning - 6th Grade Math State Test Prep Workbook |
Two Online Grade 6 Math Practice Tests & Learning Resources

**Grade 6**

### Lumos Learning
*Step Up Your Skills*

# TEST MASTERY
# Mathematics
### Boost State Assessment Scores

**30+ Skills**

((( tedBook )))

**Online Access Includes**

- 2 Full-Length Practice Tests
- Answers & Detailed Explanations
- Personalized Study Plan & Resources
- Automated Scoring and Instant Feedback

See Your Current Proficiency level & Compare With Peers

Made in the USA
Columbia, SC
17 February 2025